Under Fives – Alive!

Under Fives – Alive!

JANE FARLEY, EILEEN GODDARD AND JUDY JARVIS

Illustrations by Richard Warren

A partnership between the Methodist Church
and the National Society/Church House Publishing

National Society/Church House Publishing
Church House
Great Smith Street
London SW1P 3NZ

ISBN 0 7151 4886 9

Published 1997 by the National Society (Church of England) for Promoting Religious Education and Church House Publishing

Cover design by Leigh Hurlock
Printed in England by Longdunn Press Ltd, Bristol

Contents

Under Fives – Alive!

Under fives are indeed alive – alive to everything which goes on around them, learning all the time, ready to face new opportunities and new challenges. Life for them is full of excitement, even though their energy is not always channelled in the direction we would wish! *It is through all this energy and enthusiasm that young children learn.*

They learn through:

- seeing, touching, smelling, tasting, hearing
- imitating
- sharing with others
- experiencing the world around them
- discovering
- exploring
- making mistakes
- testing people and situations
- having fun.

This is true for all children, but is greatly helped by an environment of love and care, where ideas are encouraged and secure boundaries are provided.

How do young children learn about God and the wonders of the created world?

By being given the opportunity to:

- see, touch, smell, taste, hear
- imitate
- share with others
- experience the world around them
- discover
- explore
- make mistakes
- test people and situations
- have fun.

Just as all children learn in similar ways, so all children can begin to learn about God. For this to happen they need an atmosphere of love and care where God is at the centre, where ideas are encouraged and secure boundaries are provided.

Alive with Under Fives!

This book has been written for all those who work with Under Fives. It is full of ideas to help young children to learn through their own experience. The topics are all laid out in the same pattern, which aims to be user-friendly. There is something for everybody in Junior Churches, Sunday Schools, Parents' and Toddlers' groups, playgroups, nurseries, crèches and other situations.

Each topic can be 'dipped into' for use in single sessions or can be extended over a number of sessions. The ideas are meant to be jumping-off points for further discovery. Some have obvious links to the seasons of the year, special events and the Christian calendar.

At the heart of every topic is the setting. This is the opportunity for children to explore and discover for themselves. The setting should never be there just to look good (though we hope it will!) – rather, it is meant to be the stimulus to all the rest of the learning. Encourage the children to become involved as they arrive.

Practical Hints

The following suggestions are set out in the pattern which is used in each topic.

AIM

Keep the aim clearly in mind. Use it as a method of assessing the effectiveness of the session.

SETTING

Don't be daunted by some of the suggestions! Get as many other people as posssible involved. Good preparation makes for an easy but effective session. Make the setting children-friendly, where they can relax and enjoy themselves.

SHARING

Use the questions suggested in this section to encourage the children to enter into conversation. This might take place informally or with the group. Follow up with more 'open' questions (ones that do not have 'yes' or 'no' for an answer). Make sure that all the children have a chance to speak, either in the main group or in smaller groups.

PLAY

Encourage the children to use the setting in any way they want to, being interested, but not interfering, in what they are doing.

BIBLE LINK

Make the Bible come alive by building on the experiences the children have had through using the setting and through sharing together. Help them to understand that the Bible is not just a history book but is about real people who have a great deal in common with people today. The

Bible story has been written in full as a guide to how it might be told to young children. Helpful hints:

- Settle the children comfortably (preferably on the floor).
- Make sure there is eye contact with everybody.
- Try to tell the story rather than reading it.
- Do not rush.
- Remember – stories should be fun, so enjoy telling them. If you won't, ask someone else to do it.

ACTIVITIES

Offer a choice of activities. Encourage the children to work at their own pace, using their imagination. The results may not always be exactly what you had in mind, but the value for the child is in the doing.

MUSIC

Choose the songs or rhymes which suit the group. Don't worry if there is no accompanist. Remember that music and rhymes can have a very calming effect on excited children.

The Big Blue Planet (BBP) songbook (published by the Methodist Division of Education & Youth and Stainer & Bell, 1995) is suggested as a companion to this book, as it has a number of original songs suitable for Under Fives. (A cassette tape is also available.)

RHYMES

Use rhymes for fun. Children love rhythm, repetition and the sound of words.

DRAMA AND MOVEMENT

Children need to be active. The suggestions offer creative ways in which children can be physically involved.

ANOTHER STORY

These stories link the topic to the everyday experience of the children. Don't be afraid to replace them with a story from your own experience. Remember that children are fascinated by new, long words. They will not need explaining if they are used with the right intonation in the right context.

STORY BOOKS

Make a collection of children's story, picture and reference books. Ensure that they are always available in a quiet corner, created by a rug and a few cushions. Is your group registered to borrow a book box from your local library?

PRAYERS

Prayer time is very important. Make sure that it is imaginative and creative. It is essential to help young children to experience an atmosphere of awe and wonder in worship. (It is a great help to have a low table to gather round. Use a chipboard display table, cut down, or an upturned stacking plastic box. Cover with a cloth, changing the colour and texture as appropriate.)

PREPARATION

All the settings and many of the other activities require preparation (and clearing up). Good relationships with the caretaker are worth cultivating! Listed under [P] for Preparation are items which require major preparation or things which the parents of the children need to be warned of in advance.

What next?

Over to you! And when you've exhausted all the topics, try some of your own!

Acknowledgements

The authors and publisher gratefully acknowledge permission to reproduce copyright material in this book. Every effort has been made to trace and contact copyright holders. If there are any inadvertent omissions we apologise to those concerned. Page numbers refer to page numbers in this book.

'Five little Easter eggs' (p. 43), reproduced with permission from *Word Play, Finger Play*, Pre-School Alliance, 1985. For a full catalogue of Pre-school Learning Alliance publications and teaching resources, send an SAE to the National Centre, 69 Kings Cross Road, London WC1X 9LL.

'Fred Bumble' (p. 11) from Linda Hammond, *Five Furry Teddy Bears*, Penguin Books, 1990. Text copyright Linda Hammond 1990. Reproduced by permission of Penguin Books Ltd.

'I love the sun' (p. 87) by Gwen F. Smith, from *Someone's Singing, Lord*. By permission of Chansitor Publications Ltd, Norwich.

'Mix a pancake' (p. 83), from *Come Follow Me*, HarperCollins Publishers, originally published by Evans Bros Ltd, 1966.

'The snowman' (p. 79) by 6-year-old children at Glyn Corrwg Primary School, Glamorgan, in a poetry workshop led by Gillian Clarke. Published in *Another Very First Poetry Book*, Oxford University Press, 1992.

'What does the clock in the hall say?' (p.71) from Linda Chesterman, *Music for the Nursery School*. Reprinted by permission of Chamber Harrap Ltd.

This Little Puffin, this collection copyright © Elizabeth Matterson 1969, published by Puffin Books, Penguin Books Ltd.

Abbreviations

BBP   *Big Blue Planet*, Methodist Division
of Education & Youth and Stainer & Bell, 1995

FG   Peter Churchill, *Feeling Good*, National
Society/Church House Publishing, 1994

HPPA   Harrow Pre-School Playgroups Association

JU   *Jump Up if You're Wearing Red*, National
Society/Church House Publishing, 1996

Books

Library

BIBLE STORIES IN PICTURES

Setting

LIBRARY AREA

- Display a variety of children's books as if it were a library. Include a song-book and a tape. (Put a sheet of paper in each book.)
- Provide library equipment – e.g. a date stamp, a stamp pad, tickets, a telephone etc.
- A laptop computer.
- A typewriter.

TELLING STORIES AREA

- A rug or carpet, bean bags and cushions.
- Someone reading stories.
- Toys and pictures which relate to stories, e.g. The Three Bears, Postman Pat, Thomas the Tank Engine etc.
- A tape recorder with a story-telling tape and a linked book.

BIBLE AREA

- A large church or family Bible.
- A modern translation with pictures.
- A tiny Bible.
- A scroll.
- A child's Bible.
- A variety of children's Bible story books, including pop-up books, Bible sticker play, Little Fish books, press-out books, etc.
- Children's prayer books.
- Zig-zag Bible books.

Sharing

Ask the children to talk about and preferably show their favourite book. Why do they like the story? What's the best bit? Where did the book come from?

Play

Use the setting and everything in it.

Bible story

ACTS 8. 26–39

Worka was a long way from his home. He had driven his master from Ethiopia to Jerusalem, and now it was time to start the journey back.

Worka didn't drive a car, because there weren't any cars in those days – he drove an open chariot pulled by horses. Because Worka's master was a very important man his chariot was quite a large, comfortable one with seats in it. Even so, it would be a bumpy ride, because the chariot wheels didn't have tyres like our cars and bicycles do, and the roads then were rough and stony.

When they started out towards home, Worka's master, who was called Heili Bayissa, had a book in his hand. He said it was a very special book that he had found in Jerusalem and it was very interesting. He wanted to find out more and more about it, so he would try and read it out loud as they went along.

Soon they were out in the desert where it was hot and dusty on the rough road. Heili read the book out very slowly, but it was so hard to understand. 'I just wish there was someone who could explain it to me,' he said. 'But I don't think that will happen on this empty desert road.' Certainly there were very few people about.

Then Worka spotted someone in the distance. 'Here's a man coming,' he said. 'Wouldn't it be great if he could help us?'

To their surprise, the man waved for them to stop the chariot, and he could help them! His name was Philip and he was one of the disciples of Jesus. He climbed into the chariot beside Heili, and together they read the part of the book that was so hard. Philip told them it was about Jesus and how he could make people happy. Heili decided there and then that he wanted to be a friend of Jesus. Perhaps Worka did too?

So after they had thanked Philip and said goodbye to him they went on their way very happily.

Activities

- Make a zig-zag book (or books) from folded card. Ask each child to draw a picture and include it in the book(s).
- Provide a variety of rubber stamps and stamping pads or vegetables and thick paint on foam pads for printing. Make a book of the children's work by punching holes and tying the pages together.

Music and rhymes

SONGS

'Playing, running, skipping, jumping' (last verse) (*BBP*)

Sing these verses to the tune of 'Caring, sharing' (*BBP*):

Reading (reading), Listening (listening)
Thinking (thinking), Sharing (sharing)
Living the Jesus way.

Looking (looking), Hearing (hearing)
Laughing (laughing), Together (together)
Living the Jesus way.

RHYMES

Big books
Bright books
Bold books
Bulky books
Beautiful books
Babies' books
Bed-time books
Books, books, books.

I made a scrap book
All about me
With pictures of our home
And all the family.

I like the one of me
When I was very small,
Soon there'll be another one
When I'm really tall.

I keep it safe at home
And when I'm feeling sad
The pictures remind me
Of all the fun I've had.

Drama and movement

Act out:

- Carrying piles of books – small and big.
- Climbing steps to reach the top shelf.
- Turning pages – large movements.
- Reading a book – just moving eyes.

Another story

'How do the people in the library remember where all the books are?' Jack asked his mother. 'There are hundreds and hundreds of them in here!'

'Your Uncle John is a librarian and he's coming to supper tonight, so you can ask him,' said Mum.

'Can we ask him to read us our bed-time stories as well?' asked Jack. 'I'm sure he'll be good at that.'

'I'll have my favourite Angus book,' said little Alice. 'The one when he got lost.'

'You always choose that one,' laughed Mum. 'I'm sure you know it off by heart.'

Jack wasn't sure which book he would have, there were so many that he liked.

When Jack and Alice were ready for bed, Uncle John came up to the bedroom. 'I'm ready,' he said. 'What shall we do first?' Jack told him Mum always sang nursery rhymes before they had their stories. 'Fine,' said Uncle John. 'How about "Baa-baa black hen, have you any eggs?" Or "Humpty-Dumpty sat on the bed"?'

'No, no!' shouted the children. 'That's wrong, it's silly.'

Mum came up to see what was happening. She joined in with 'Little Jack Horner sat on the bus' and 'Hickory, dickory dock, the cow ran up the clock'. Soon they were all laughing until Mum said it was time to settle down.

Alice gave Uncle John her favourite book, *Angus Lost*, about a little black dog getting lost in the snow and finding his way home, when he heard the milkman. She loved the bit, 'Rattle, rattle, clink, clink, here comes the milkman'. Funny Uncle John got it wrong again at first. He called Angus 'Agnes' and

said it was the dustman Angus heard going 'Crash, crash, thump, thump'. But then he read her book to her properly and she was so happy. Soon she was fast asleep.

Uncle John told Jack about his job as a librarian and how he had computers and machines to help him remember where all the books were. Then he got out a lovely book he'd found for Jack, to read him a story. It was called *Tales of the River Bank* about Ratty, Mole, Toad and Mr Badger. Jack thought they were super stories and he loved the pictures of the four animals and the river.

'When you're older, you can read the whole book that these stories come from – it's called *The Wind in the Willows*,' said Uncle John. 'There are so many books waiting for you to read, you know.'

Story books

Everything!

Cherry Gilchrist. *A Visit to the Library*. Cambridge Books for Children, 1984.

Prayers

Ask each child to choose a book, put it in the middle and then sit down in a circle. Read a prayer from a children's prayer book. Thank God for books, particularly the Bible.

Clothes

Aim

To help children to appreciate clothes, both theirs and other people's, but to understand that they are not all-important

Setting

Different sorts of clothes in each area of the room:

HEADGEAR

Hats (adults' and children's, male and female), scarves, sporting hats (e.g. riding helmets), bridal head-dresses, workers' head-gear (e.g. nurse, police officer, chauffeur, sailor, soldier etc.), headgear from other countries (e.g. American Indian head-dresses), paper crowns and other paper hats.

FOOTWEAR

Boots and shoes (adults' and children's), specialist footwear (ballet, riding, football, flippers, slippers, roller skates etc.).

HANDWEAR

Gloves (rubber, plastic, gardening, evening, winter, mittens, oven, golf etc.), handbags (all sizes and shapes).

BODYWEAR

Lower half (large children's or small adults') – trousers, shorts, leggings, swimming-trunks, skirts, jodphurs; top half (large children's or small adults') – jackets, shirts, jumpers, blouses, capes, shawls.

ALL OVER

Bodysuits, dresses, saris, African and Asian clothes.

Sharing

Why do we wear clothes? What sort of clothes do we wear in cold/hot/wet weather? What are your favourites? What is different between the clothes you wear and the clothes grown-ups wear?

Play

Give the children free rein to dress up in the clothes. Encourage those who are hesitant. Talk to the children about what they are doing and who they are pretending to be as they dress up. It is fun for adults to dress up as well.

Bible story
MATTHEW 6. 25–32

What do you think it was like to live when Jesus did? There are lots of stories about Jesus and his friends, the disciples, and we know that they didn't stay in one place very long. Instead they kept moving from one village to another, staying in people's houses and getting to know them.

There were no cars, buses or bicycles, so they walked everywhere and carried what they needed with them. It was a hot country, so they didn't need a lot of clothes, but even these needed washing and mending sometimes, and there were no washing machines or irons. They had bone needles and thread for their mending, but the clothes had to be washed and scrubbed on the rocks in the rivers and dried in the sun.

Some of the disciples got rather worried that their clothes were getting worn out. One day they were talking about this as they walked through the fields. Suddenly they saw a patch of bright coloured flowers which looked lovely.

- Make sock puppets for the children to use. Fasten on two buttons for eyes, adding ears, a tongue, teeth and earrings, as required.
- Provide each child with a simple crown shape, for them to decorate with paper, fabric, sequins etc.
- Play 'Hunt the Slipper'.

Music and rhymes

SONGS

'Always remember, never forget' (*BBP*)

'Dashing away with the smoothing iron' (*Traditional*)

'Playing, running, skipping, jumping' (*BBP* and *JU*)

RHYMES

I can tie my shoe lace
I can brush my hair
I can wash my hands and face
And dry myself with care.
I can clean my teeth too
Fasten up my frocks
I can say 'How do you do'
And pull up both my socks.

HPPA

'Look at them,' said Jesus. 'What wonderful colours! How do the flowers grow like that?'

Nathaniel replied, 'They just grow.'

'Yes,' said Jesus. 'They don't have to worry at all; God takes care of them. So we shouldn't worry too much about our clothes, because God takes care of us.'

'Those bright colours look good on the flowers,' Peter said. 'I'm not too sure they'd look good on us, though – people might think we were showing off.'

Soon they were all laughing as they imagined themselves in bright red, blue and purple clothes. 'People would see us coming and they might think we were very important,' said John. 'Then they would be afraid to talk to us.'

Jesus agreed with him. 'We want everyone to be able to talk to us and to be our friends, no matter what clothes we wear.'

Big brown boots go
Tramp, tramp, tramp.
Little red shoes go
Stamp, stamp, stamp.
Silver slippers go
Trip, trip, trip.
And my two feet go
Skip, skip, skip.

HPPA

Activities

- On large sheets of paper, draw round one or more of the children and cut out the shape. Alternatively supply cut-out shapes to the children, at least 40 centimetres high. Provide them with fabric or coloured paper pre-cut into randomly shaped pieces. Encourage the children to dress the shapes by sticking on the pieces with PVA glue.

Jennie Muddlecombe has lost her hat
She can't find it anywhere, well fancy that.
She walked down the High Street and everybody said,
'Funny old Jennie Muddlecombe, her hat is on her head.'

HPPA

Drama and movement

Suggest to the children different kinds of shoes and boots (e.g. wellingtons, high heels, tap shoes, football boots, climbing boots). Ask them to move around as if they are wearing them. Ask them to do the same wearing different hats (e.g. jockey's cap, crash helmet, riding hat, soldier's helmet).

Another story

It was the day before Anne's wedding, so the house was full of people, all very busy getting things ready for the next day. They were lifting clothes out of boxes and getting them out of cupboards, to be ironed and hung up. There were the pretty flowered dresses of the bridesmaids, Anne's lovely wedding dress and veil, Mum's new outfit and hat, and Dad's suit.

It was so busy in the house that Dad had gone into the garden to cut the grass and to do a bit of digging. Suddenly Mum came to the back door and called out, 'What trousers have you got on?'

'My old green gardening pair of course,' Dad replied. 'Why do you want to know?'

Mum seemed quite worried. 'I've got your best suit out of the cupboard and there's only the jacket on the hanger, no trousers. Do you know where they are?'

Dad said he'd no idea, but he'd come and look. He searched through his cupboard and everyone else's cupboards, but they weren't there. Then other people joined in the search, but it was no good, and soon everyone was worried – except Anne. She was laughing. 'You'll have to walk me up the church aisle in your best jacket and your old green gardening trousers, Dad,' she said. 'Then everyone

will remember my wedding!' Soon everyone was laughing and thinking of the un-wedding things they could wear – their aprons or their wellies or their crash helmets.

Just then the door-bell rang and when Mum opened the door, Gran was standing there with Dad's best trousers hanging over her arm. She was surprised to find them all laughing and even more surprised when they all shouted, 'Hooray! The trousers are here!'

Gran explained that she'd noticed a button that was loose when Dad had last worn them and she'd taken the trousers home to sew the button on properly. Then she'd forgotten to bring them back. How pleased everyone was. Anne gave Dad a hug. 'I'm glad we've found your trousers,' she said. 'But it's you I want at my wedding, and I really wouldn't mind what you wore – even those old green gardening trousers!'

Story books

- Mary Dickinson, *New Clothes for Alex*, Hippo, 1984.
- Pat Hutchins, *You'll Soon Grow Into Them Titch*, Red Fox, 1984.
- Debbie Bailey, *Clothes*, Annick Press, 1991.
- Debbie Bailey, *Hats*, Annick Press, 1991.
- Sarah Garland, *Doing the Washing*, Picture Puffins, 1988.

Prayers

Ask the children to choose an item of clothing, then to sit in a circle. Thank God for clothes to wear in different kinds of weather (e.g. hot, cold, wet, snow). Ask the children to place the appropriate clothes in the centre before each prayer.

Where we live

Aim

To help children to realise how fortunate they are to have homes

Setting

Use each corner of the room to represent a different area of the house:

KITCHEN

A washing-up bowl and mop, plates and a rack, cups and saucers, plastic bowls, washing-up liquid, an electric toaster and bread, some food items in tins and jars, a dustpan and brush, liquid detergent and dirty washing, a clothes rack, some utensils (e.g. a colander, cake tins, saucepans), tea towels.

LIVING ROOM

An easy chair, a rug, cushions, a television set or radio, a clock, newspapers, magazines, comics and books, pot plants, ornaments, framed photographs.

BEDROOM

A camp bed with duvet, sheets and pillows, a travelling cot (and dolls to put in it), a bedside light, a hair brush and comb, toys, books (both adults' and children's), an alarm clock, coat hangers with clothes, a mirror, make-up, a soft toy.

BATHROOM

Towels, face-cloths, soap, a toothbrush, toothpaste, a tooth-mug, a toilet brush, a toilet roll, a potty, a child's toilet seat, a bath mat, a pedestal mat, a linen basket.

Note: Resist the temptation to use child-sized items which are usually found in a home corner. On this occasion there needs to be a feeling of realism.

Sharing

Where do you live? What is the name of your town? What is the name of your road? Who else lives in your house? Which is your favourite place in your house? Where do you go if you are feeling sad?

Play

Use the setting and everything in it to act out being at home. Do some washing up. Do some washing. Hang the clothes out to dry. Have a tooth-cleaning session [P]. Watch a cartoon from the *Children's Video Bible* or *Hippety Dog*.

Bible story
LUKE 9. 58

Thaddaeus and James had been friends for a long time. When they were little boys they lived near each other and often played together. Then they went to the same school. When they were older they met nearly every day to talk about what they wanted to do – what sort of work and how they would spend their time.

One morning Thaddaeus had some interesting news: he had heard from his cousin Jacob from the next village about a man called Jesus who had arrived there the day before. He was talking to lots of people and telling them wonderful stories. 'He's actually coming here tomorrow,' said Thaddaeus. 'Let's go and hear him for ourselves.'

Next day Thaddaeus and James were sitting in the crowd of people waiting for Jesus to come and talk to them. He arrived with a few friends. People were surprised that they were all quite young men (rather like Thaddeus and James). Then Jesus started talking, and his voice made everyone listen very carefully

and quietly. What he said was so exciting that Thaddeus and James could hardly wait to go and talk to him themselves.

The two of them went up to Jesus and asked if they could join him and his friends on their travels. Jesus explained that it would be a hard life, because they would always be moving on from one place to another and wouldn't have a home to go to every night. 'Foxes have holes and birds have nests,' he said. 'But I never know where I am going to sleep.'

He was right – it was a hard life, but Thaddaeus and James were always pleased that they had gone with Jesus and become his disciples.

Activities

- A sorting game [P].
- Make up 'pretend' beds on the floor with blankets, and encourage the children to have a five-minute sleep session – if possible!

Music and rhymes

SONGS

'Caring, sharing' (*BBP*)

'Always remember, never forget' (*BBP*)

'This is the way we clean our teeth, wash the clothes, mop the floor, hoover the carpet, go to bed . . .' (and any other appropriate variations)

Old Fred Bumble had a bath,
He had lots of fun.
He would turn both taps on full,
And watch the water run.

Chorus
With a splash, splash here,
And a splash, splash there,
Here a splash, there a splash
Everywhere a splash, splash.
When Old Fred Bumble had a bath
He had lots of fun.

When Old Fred Bumble had a bath,
Water to the top.
Higher, higher, watch it come,
Would it ever stop?

Chorus

When Old Fred Bumble had a bath
He'd wash from head to toe.
Then he'd pull the plug right out
And watch the water go.

Linda Hammond, in Five Furry Teddy Bears

(To the tune of 'Old Macdonald had a farm'.)

This little girl is ready for bed,
On her pillow she lays her head,
Wraps herself in her duvet tight,
Closes her eyes and says 'Goodnight'.

(To the tune of 'Here we go round the mulberry bush'.)

RHYMES

Build the house up very high,
Point the chimneys to the sky,
Put the roof on, lay the floor,
Open wide the big front door.

Traditional

(Use actions.)

 ## Drama and movement

Acting out the song 'This is the way'.

Miming and guessing which room it is (e.g. getting into bed).

Another story

Carol and Jim were going with Mum to take the flowers from church to a lady who wasn't very well. Miss Simpson lived in a block of flats just round the corner. When they got there, they found they had to press the bell and speak into a sort of box on the wall. After a bit, they heard a voice asking them who they were, so Mum explained.

'Please come in through the door when it makes a buzzing noise,' said Miss Simpson's voice. 'Then you can come up in the lift to the second floor. My door is the blue one and I'll be waiting for you.'

Jim pressed the buttons in the lift, and up they went and found the blue door. Miss Simpson was quite an old lady, and she couldn't move about very well. She was sitting in her chair with a bright warm rug over her knees.

She was so pleased to see them and she was delighted to have the flowers from the people at church. While Mum arranged these in a vase, Miss Simpson said Carol and Jim could have a good look round her flat. They saw some things that were rather different from their home. In the kitchen there were some funny taps with long handles. Miss Simpson said that you could even turn them on with your elbows, so Carol and Jim had a go. Beside her bed, as well as next to her chair in the sitting room, there was a sort of telephone with a big red button.

Jim looked in the bathroom. That was interesting – there was a special seat that fitted in the bath and another high seat on the toilet. This had rails round it to hold on to so that you could stand up easily.

Why are there two long cord light switches in here?' he asked.

Miss Simpson called out, 'Please don't pull them, because one of them will make a bell ring in the office, and the lady who looks after us will come running up to see what is the matter! That's what the big red button on the telephone is for, as well.'

Then they all laughed. 'There are a lot of buttons and switches in these flats,' said Carol.

Miss Simpson said, 'Nearly all the people who live here find some things that are hard for them to do by themselves, so they need someone to come and help. But we do have to remember which is the right button to press each time.'

Story books

Shirley Hughes, *Moving Molly*, Walker Books, 1978.

Brian Wildsmith, *Animal Homes*, Oxford University Press, 1991.

Debi Gliori, *New Big House*, Walker Books, 1994.

Anne Civardi, *Moving House*, Usborne, 1992.

Prayers

Gather in a circle. Place in the centre some items collected from the corners of the setting and a very large cardboard box, an old blanket and some newspapers. Ask the children why the cardboard box is there. Explain that some people (including children) have no homes and have to sleep in boxes in the streets. Say prayers of thanks for homes and families. Remember those who have no home. Ask God to care for them. Pray that other people will help them to find somewhere to live.

Preparation

- Ask the children to bring their toothbrushes (labelled).
- Make up a sorting game. Cut out pictures from magazines and catalogues to represent items from different rooms in a house. Stick them on to card. Ask the children to sort them into the rooms in which they belong.

Transport

Aim

To help children to think about different kinds of transport and to be more aware of those who take them safely on their journeys

Booking Office

Setting

Use each corner of the room to represent a different type of transport:

ROAD

- A floor mat, with road furniture and miniature cars, buses, trucks, lorries, diggers.
- A garage.
- Duplo Lego.
- Play-people figures (e.g. policeman, road mender).

RAILWAY

- A wooden or plastic railway, trains etc.
- A station.
- An electric train set, with owner!

AIRPORT [P]

- Wooden, metal or plastic toy planes.
- A Fisher-Price airport terminal.

HARBOUR

- A plastic bath, paddling pool or water bath from a playgroup, with boats, yachts and ships.
- A floating harbour made from a piece of polystyrene where the boats can be moored.

IN THE CENTRE

- A small table to become a booking office.

- A pile of small pieces of paper for tickets.
- A stamp and stamp pads for marking the tickets.
- Timetables.
- Bus and Tube maps.
- Dressing-up hats (e.g. driver's, pilot's, sailor's, crash helmet, cycle helmet).

ON THE WALLS

- Pictures and friezes.

Sharing

Who has been on a boat? What kind was it? Where were you going? What did you do on/in it? Repeat for the other forms of transport.

Play

Play in the settings.

Bible story
ACTS 27

Paul had a very important job, travelling all over the world, telling people about Jesus. Sometimes he walked, sometimes he rode on a horse or on a camel, and quite often he went on ships. They weren't big ferries like there are today, they were small sailing ships, which zipped along the water when there was a good wind behind them. Paul loved those days; he stood up on the deck and watched the sun sparkling on the water and listened to the wind whistling around the ropes and sails.

But there came a day when the weather changed. There were dark clouds, no sunshine at all, and it poured with rain and the wind howled round the ship. The sailors couldn't put the sails up, because the wind just tore them to pieces.

This meant the ship could only go where the wind blew it, and after a few days no one knew where they were.

Sometimes Paul could hardly stand up on the deck of the ship, and the sailors had to hold on really tight when they were up there. There was always someone on look-out, clinging to the ropes at the top of the mast.

Suddenly he shouted, 'Land ho, I can see land!'

The captain said, 'I've no idea what land that is, but I'm going to try and get there. We'll have to find a way in for our ship, without hitting any rocks or sand banks.'

The sailors used a long line with a weight on the end. They managed to hold on to one end of the line and drop the rest over the side. It was not easy on a ship that was tossing up and down. Each time they pulled the line up, they measured how deep the water was. Twenty fathoms, next time fifteen fathoms, next time eleven fathoms. That was worrying. But now they could see a sandy bay where the water seemed calmer and the wind didn't seem to be blowing so hard.

'I'm going in there!' shouted the captain. 'Get ready, everyone – there may be a big bump.' There was, and also a horrible cracking, grinding noise, as the ship ran on to the sand. 'Jump out and swim for the shore if you can,' called the captain. 'Or find a piece of wood and paddle your way in.'

When everyone was off the ship, the captain lined them all up and counted them. Everyone was there. Paul said, 'Let's all give thanks to God that we are safe here.'

Activities

● Make junk models.
● Provide large brushes and ready-mixed paint for a painting activity.

Music and rhymes

Songs

'Riding in a car on the motorway' (*BBP*)

'One day when we were fishing' (*BBP*)

'With Jesus in the boat' (*Junior Praise*)

'The wheels on the bus' (*Traditional*)

'Row, row, row the boat' (*Traditional*)

Rhymes

I had a little motor car,
My motor wouldn't go.
I had to push and push and push
And still it wouldn't go.

I had a little engine,
My engine wouldn't go.
I had to pull and pull and pull
And still it wouldn't go.

I had a little aeroplane,
My aeroplane would fly.
Away it flew, into the air
High into the sky.

HPPA

Drama and movement

Mime any kind of activity to do with transport.

Another story

There was a special notice fixed on Julie and John's Mum's car because she was learning to drive. It was a white square with a big red 'L' on it. Mum's name was Lorraine but she said the 'L' was not for her name but because she was a learner.

Then one day she came home very happy indeed. 'I've passed my driving test!' she said, 'so I can take the red "L" off the car because I'm not a learner any more. I can put a green "L" on my car for a year, and then everyone will know I've only just stopped being a learner.'

Next time they all went out in their car with Mum driving, Julie and John were on the look-out for red 'L's on people's cars. One was on a yellow car, going very slowly, and Mum said that was probably a very new learner like she used to be. Then there was a motor-bike with a red 'L'; it was next to them at the traffic lights.

'Gosh,' said John. 'You have to learn to drive a motor-bike, do you? That's what I'd like to have one day.'

Just then a big lorry came round the corner with red 'L's on it. 'How about that for you, Julie? Would you like to be a lorry driver when you grow up?' said Dad. But Julie said she really wanted to be an engine driver. No one was sure whether trains had red 'L's on them, but they were sure people did have to learn to drive railway engines.

Soon after that the family were going on holiday – on an aeroplane for the first time, so that was really exciting. At the airport, they checked their luggage in and then they had to wait a bit in a room called the departure lounge for their plane. Julie and John were standing by the window watching planes landing and taking off. They saw their plane come slowly round the end of the building to stop at the bottom of the steps.

'Oh look,' they said, almost together, 'our plane has a big red "L" on its side. Do you think our pilot is a learner?'

Everyone laughed and Dad explained that the 'L' on the plane was part of its own registration number and not for a learner at all. 'You can see some numbers after the "L", so we needn't worry – our pilot has passed his driving test to fly aeroplanes.'

Then there was an announcement. It was time to go – down a slope, through some doors, across the tarmac, up the steep steps and into the plane.

Story books

- Philippe Dupasquier, *A Busy Day at the Garage, Airport, Harbour, Railway Station*, Walker, 1994.
- Jon Blake, *Impo*, Walker, 1994.
- Anne Rockwell, *Cars*, Picture Puffin, 1988.

 ## Prayers

Set some chairs out to look like the inside of a bus, train, tube or plane, with an empty seat for the driver. Sit in the seats. Say prayers for the drivers, pilots etc. who take us safely on our journeys.

Preparation

Make a simple airport 'mat' with runways, a control tower and terminal buildings.

New babies

Setting

- A cradle or carry-cot, and a carry-chair or a pram, buggy or push-chair – both real ones and toy ones.
- Blankets, sheets, bedcovers, quilts etc.
- Baby dolls (multi-ethnic, male and female) and choices of clothes.
- A baby bath, a changing bag/mat with equipment, nappies, a baby's bottle.
- Low chairs.
- Baby toys.
- Pictures of the children as young babies and of babies in their families [P].

Sharing

Does anyone know someone with a new baby? Whose baby is it? Tell us something about the baby. What can babies do? What can't they do? What do we have to do for them?

Play

Play at being mothers and fathers, sisters and brothers within the setting.

Bible story

EXODUS 2. 1–10

'What are we going to do with him? He is a beautiful baby. We must think of a way to hide him away from the soldiers who want to kill all the little boy babies.'

For three months they kept him hidden in the house, but as he began to grow he made a lot more noise when he cried. So his mother decided she would make a special cradle, like a big basket. She would make it watertight and use reeds from the river bank for the outside. It would then float in the reeds by the edge of the river. The soldiers would never think of looking there.

His sister Miriam spent every day sitting by the river close to the cradle – keeping watch. One day the king's daughter, the princess, came down to the river for a swim. 'Oh dear,' thought Miriam, 'I hope the baby doesn't make a noise!' Guess what! He did! He was hungry, and he started to cry loudly.

The princess heard it and sent her ladies-in-waiting to bring the baby to her. They lifted the basket out of the river, took it to her and put it carefully down on the bank. There inside was a lovely baby boy. 'This must be one of the Jewish children,' said the Princess. 'He is so lovely, he must not be killed.'

Miriam was very worried about what would happen. She walked nearer to the group. She could see the Princess was wondering what to do. 'Excuse me,' she said. 'Shall I go and fetch you a Jewish woman to look after the child?'

'Oh yes, if you know someone.' She ran home and fetched her mother, and the princess said she would pay her to nurse him for her.

When Moses was old enough his mother took him to the palace to the princess. She was so pleased to adopt him. 'I will call him Moses, because I took him from the water!'

Activities

- Invite parents to bring their young babies to the group [P]. Encourage the children to ask questions about the babies and to 'help' in their care.
- Look at photographs of the children as babies, and try to guess which photograph belongs to which child [P].

- Make some simple mobiles. Provide some cardboard shapes – circles, triangles, diamonds etc. Decorate them by sticking on pieces of shiny paper. Hang them from a metal coat-hanger.

Music and rhymes

SONGS

'We thank you God, for mummies' (the verse about babies) (*BBP*)

'Welcome, welcome to our family' (*BBP*)

'Rock-a-bye-baby' (*Traditional*)

RHYMES

Peek-a-boo, peek-a-boo,
Who's that hiding there?
Peek-a-boo, peek-a-boo,
(*The baby's name*)'s behind the chair.

Traditional

Drama and movement

- Act out being babies. Lie on backs, kick, explore toys, drag on tummies (if the floor is smooth and clean), crawl round the room. Take first steps (do it in groups of three, taking turns to be 'baby' and catchers).
- Play lullaby music (e.g. Brahms' 'Cradle Song') and use gentle rocking movements.

Another story

Judith often visited Mary and Jack who lived next door. One day they told her something exciting – they were going to have a baby quite soon. That was why Mary had stopped going to work. She was making one of the bedrooms ready as a nursery and had started collecting all the things the baby would need. Mary was busy every morning, but in the afternoons she had a good rest on the settee, and put her feet up. If Judith was there at Mary's, she would go back home.

'Did you do that, Mummy?' asked Judith, 'when you were getting ready for me to be your baby?' Mummy said she'd tell Judith a special story about that time. Here it is for you to listen to as well:

'Once upon a time there was a Mummy and Daddy who hadn't got a baby. They wanted one very much indeed, so they were rather sad. The doctor had told them that they were

not able to make a baby. He told them about adopting a baby whose parents couldn't look after it well enough. They needed other people to become the baby's parents. The Mummy and Daddy thought a lot about the idea, and they decided they would like to adopt a baby. They had to wait quite a long time and, like Mary and Jack next door, they got everything ready. Then one day a letter came to tell them there was a very little baby girl, who had been quite ill, ready for them to adopt. They packed the car with the carry-cot, the baby clothes, the nappies and some lovely little presents, and they set off.

'I wonder what our baby girl looks like,' said Mummy.

'I don't know,' Daddy said. 'But I know she is going to be very special.'

As soon as they saw her in the nursery, they both said, 'She is very special, and she is going to be lovely, our little Judith.'

This story is about you, Judith, and I'll tell you something else that is exciting: we are going to adopt another baby as soon as we can, who will be your little brother or sister.'

Judith was very excited. She could hardly wait to go and tell the special story to Mary and Jack next door. One day she'd be able to tell the special story to her own little brother or sister too.

Story books

- Babette Cole, *Mummy Laid an Egg*, Red Fox, 1996.
- Anne Civardi and Stephen Cartwright, *The New Baby*, Usbourne First Experiences, 1992.
- Bob Graham, *The Red Woollen Blanket*, Walker, 1988.
- Anthea Sieverking. *The Baby's Book of Babies*, Windward, 1988

Prayers

If possible, gather in a circle round a visiting mother and baby. Alternatively, invite the children to form a circle, holding dolls as babies. Have a few moments of 'hush'. Look at the baby or dolls. Thank God for babies, for their fingers, toes and tiny noses. Sing 'He's got the whole world in his hands', including 'He's got the tiny little baby in his hands'.

Preparation

- Invite parents and babies to visit.
- Arrange for photographs of the children as babies to be brought in.
- If possible, obtain bulrushes and a baby basket.

Grandparents

Aim

*To help children
to think about their
grandparents,
wherever they are.*

Setting

- A wide variety of clothes for dressing up, including skirts, blouses, shirts, cardigans, jackets, trousers, hats (male and female), sweaters and anoraks. Also scarves, beads, handbags, spectacles (without lenses) and a camera.
- Walking boots, walking sticks, umbrellas.
- Newspapers, magazines, holiday and garden catalogues.
- Knitting, sewing, a telephone, a wheelbarrow, a trowel, flower pots, a spade, novels.
- Paper, pens, envelopes, stamps.
- Photographs of the children's grandparents [P].

Sharing

What do you call your grandparents? Where do they live? What games do they play with you? Do they have some special toys for you to play with? Most children have something special they like to do with their grandparents – what is yours? What do you think they do when you're not there?

Play

Use the setting and everything in it to act out being grandparents.

Bible story

LUKE 2. 21–35

Simeon was an old man and he was not very well. He lived by himself in Jerusalem. It took him quite a long time to walk anywhere, and then he needed to sit down and rest.

The one place he tried to walk to every day was the Temple, the big church in the middle of Jerusalem. He liked to find a seat in a cool, shady part of the Temple, where he could sit and watch the people coming in and out.

Simeon watched their faces; he wondered why they were there and what they were thinking about.

The people he enjoyed watching most of all were fathers and mothers bringing a new baby to be blessed by the priests. They looked so proud. If the baby was quiet, then the parents seemed happy. If the baby was crying they seemed quite worried. Then Simeon said, 'Don't worry! Babies cry in your house sometimes. This Temple is God's house and I'm sure he won't mind.'

That usually cheered them up and they said, 'What a lovely grandfather you must be – you are so understanding.' Then Simeon smiled: he didn't have any grandchildren of his own, so all these babies were special to him.

Simeon knew that one day he would see a father and mother coming into the Temple with their baby, and this baby would be extra special. He might even feel like the baby's grandfather. How would he know? He wasn't sure. Sometimes he worried that he might get too old and ill to get himself to his seat in the Temple before this happened.

He had just arrived there one morning and was sitting down to get his breath back. He had walked a bit more quickly than usual because it was cold and windy. He looked up and saw a father and mother with their baby standing quietly in front of him. Everyone smiled as if they had always known each other and as if Simeon really was this baby's grandfather. He was so happy. He knew for sure that this was the extra-special baby he had been waiting to see.

'Please tell me your names,' he said, 'and the name of your baby too.'

The father replied, 'We're Joseph and Mary, and this is Jesus.'

Mary put the baby gently into Simeon's arms and said, 'Please will you bless him?'

Simeon said some prayers, thanking God for baby Jesus, who would grow up to be the special person that everyone had been waiting for. He said his own thank-you prayer because he had been able to see Jesus for himself.

Then he said to Joseph and Mary, 'You are special too, because you are the father and mother of Jesus. I know you'll look after him well. Sometimes you'll be sad when bad things happen to him, but in the end his love for everyone will make you happy too.'

Simeon knew now that he didn't have to come to the Temple every day. He could rest when he wanted to, at home. He was really happy.

Activities

- Make a card for grandparents – not just for Christmas and birthdays, perhaps a 'Looking forward to seeing you' card. (Use collage or free drawing, giving the children the opportunity to do as much as possible for themselves.)
- Invite a grandparent into the group, bringing pictures of their grandchildren to share. They may also have a hobby which they could show to the children.
- Invite the older members of the congregation in to share a drink and biscuits.
- Go as a group to take a plant to an elderly housebound person.

Music and rhymes

SONGS

'We thank you God for mummies' (*BBP*) (change to 'We thank you God for grandmas/pas' etc.)

'Helping Grandma Jones' (verses only) (*Tinderbox*)

RHYMES

Here are grandma's spectacles
Here is grandma's hat
This is the way she folds her hands
And puts them in her lap.

Here are grandad's glasses
Here is grandad's hat
This is the way he folds his arms
And takes a little nap.

Are your grandparents like this? Or are they more like this?

Here are grandma's walking boots
Here's her big briefcase
This is how she drives the car
As she goes from place to place.

Here are grandad's golf clubs
Here's his new walkman
This is how he goes for the train
Running as fast as he can.

Traditional, adapted

Drama and movement

- Sing with actions to the tune of 'A-hunting we will go':

This is what we do (x3)
When Grandad/Granny comes to stay

We go out for a walk (x3)
When Grandad/Granny comes to stay.

We build a big bonfire (x3)
We sit and look at books (x3)
We have a cup of tea (x3)
We play exciting games (x3)

Another story

Meg's grandparents had come to stay at her house for two nights while her Mum and Dad went to an important meeting. They told Granny and Grandad that Meg would not be any trouble at all, except perhaps in the morning, when she couldn't make up her mind about what clothes she would wear.

'We'll manage somehow,' said Grandad. They all waved goodbye to Mum and Dad.

When it was time for bath, bed and a story, Granny asked Meg to find her pyjamas. 'Oh, that's easy,' said Meg.

On Friday morning it was easy too, because Granny and Grandad were taking Meg swimming, and she always wore her tracksuit to go to the pool, like Granny and Grandad, so that they were all the same.

But on Saturday morning, when Meg woke up, she couldn't decide what to wear. Granny got out her blue pinafore dress, and her red trousers, and the striped shirt, and then her black leggings, and the flower top – none of them would do!

'OK,' said Granny, 'if you can't decide what to put on, you'd better stay in your pyjamas and your dressing-gown.'

Meg was quite pleased to have her breakfast in them and to wear them when she played with her building bricks and her puzzles, while Granny and Grandad tidied around and washed up.

Then they decided to do a bit of gardening. 'Oh, can I come too?' said Meg. 'I like gardening.' But she'd only got her pyjamas and dressing-gown on, so she couldn't go out.

Later on Granny and Grandad thought about going for a walk to post a letter, but they couldn't take Meg because she was still in her pyjamas and dressing-gown. So they all stayed in.

At dinner time Grandad said, 'What a pity we can't go for an outing this afternoon, perhaps we could have gone to feed the ducks.'

'We might have been able to have a picnic too – it's such a lovely day,' said Granny. 'But we can't go if you're wearing just pyjamas and a dressing-gown!'

Meg thought hard. 'If I put on my red trousers and a warm jumper, could we go?'

'Why yes,' they said. 'Maybe wearing your pyjamas and dressing-gown all the time isn't much fun, is it?'

When Mum and Dad came home Meg told them she'd had a lovely time with Granny and Grandad. 'I've decided it's best to wear clothes in the day and pyjamas at night.'

Everyone said 'Yes.'

What do you think?

Story books

- Sarah Keane, *My Grandma*, Mammoth, 1994.
- Brian Smith, *Do You Know What Grandad Did?*, Orchard Picture Books, 1991.
- Pat Hutchins, *The Doorbell Rang*, Picture Puffin, 1988.
- Pat Hutchins, *Happy Birthday Sam*, Picture Puffin, 1981.

Prayers

In the middle of the group put the photographs of grandparents which the children have brought [P]. Say prayers for grandparents based on the sharing session. Thank God for them.

Preparation

Photos of grandparents need to be brought in by the children or their parents.

Parties

➚ **Aim**

To encourage children not only to enjoy having a party but also to be involved in the preparation. To make them aware that not all children are able to have parties

DANDELION AND BURDOCK 2L

COLA

prawn and pickled onion flavour CRISPS

Setting

- Pre-prepared invitations. One for each child [P].

Room decoration

- Use wrapping paper on the walls as posters.
- Hang party banners, crêpe-paper chains and balloons (tie some balloons outside the door).

Table decoration

- A party tablecloth and serviettes or coloured crêpe paper.
- Party poppers.
- Plain paper plates, cups/mugs.

Food and drink

- Jugs of water, bottles of squash, crisps, small savoury biscuits, pâté (or an alternative), small cooked sausages, cubes of cheese and pineapple.
- Small sweet biscuits and ready-made icing in various colours.
- Yoghurt and puréed fruit to mix with it.

Sharing

- Who's had a birthday? What did you do to celebrate your birthday?
- What other sorts of parties have you been to? What did you do?
- Have you been to any other sorts of parties (e.g. wedding, Christmas, family, funeral, Golden Wedding)? How is a party different from an ordinary meal?

Play

- Use the setting and everything in it to prepare for a party.

- Offer a variety of materials to decorate the edges of the paper plates (e.g. paints, felt-tipped pens, sticky paper shapes).
- Spread the pâté onto the savoury biscuits.
- Ice the sweet biscuits.
- Put the cheese and pineapple and small sausages onto cocktail sticks, and stick them into halved grapefruits or oranges (or even foil-covered playdough!) to make 'hedgehogs'.
- Mix the yoghurt and puréed fruit together.

Bible story
Luke 15. 11–24

Reuben couldn't sleep. This night was not really different from lots of other nights. He would lie awake, tossing and turning because he just couldn't settle down.

The trouble was, he was worrying all the time about his son Joel, even though he was grown up now. Reuben didn't know where Joel was. They had had an awful argument last year, and Joel had left home. No one had seen him or heard from him since then. It had made Reuben very sad. He didn't know if he would ever see Joel again.

So Reuben decided to get up and find his way up the hill beside the house, where it was quiet and peaceful. Sitting up there, he watched the sun coming up, getting brighter and brighter every minute. He could see little figures down there, people setting out to work in the fields and taking their flocks of sheep to find fresh green grass. There were one or two others making their way to the well to fetch water, and there was someone coming slowly along the road that came from the town over the hill.

As this person got nearer and nearer, Reuben rubbed his eyes. Could it be? Yes, it was – it really was Joel! He jumped up and ran down to him. Before Joel could say a word, he hugged him so happily.

Joel said, 'I am so sorry about our argument, father. I didn't know whether you would want to see me again.'

Reuben said, 'You are here, and I am so happy to have you back. That's the most important thing, because I thought I might never see you again.'

Then he had a good idea. 'Let's have a party!' So they did.

Activities

- Make party hats. Use a simple strip of paper to make a crown shape. Decorate it with shapes cut from shiny paper.
- Make jelly, using a small quantity of boiling water and adding ice cubes for quick setting.
- Mix the drinks.
- Have a parcel ready-made to play 'Pass the Parcel' [P].
- Collect ideas from the children for other party games (e.g. musical bumps, musical chairs, squeak piggy squeak, dead lions, the hokey cokey). Have a cassette player and some cassettes ready [P].
- Play the games, eat the food, have a party!

Music and rhymes

Songs

'Welcome, welcome today' (*BBP*)

'Tingle, tingle, tingle' (*BBP*)

'It's birthday time' (*BBP* and *FG*)

'I like eating' (*BBP* and *FG*)

Sing to the tune of 'In and out the bluebells':

Let's all have a party (x 3)
And have a lot of fun.

We'll eat cake and jelly (x 3)
And have a lot of fun.

Let's play Pass the Parcel (x 3)
And have a lot of fun.

Traditional, adapted

(*Make up more verses as required.*)

Jelly on a plate
Jelly on a plate
Wibble wobble, wibble wobble
Jelly on a plate.

Sausage in a pan
Sausage in a pan
Sizzle, sizzle, sizzle, sizzle
Sausage in a pan.

Traditional, adapted

Drama and movement

The games will provide all that is needed.

Story

A letter came to Josie and Mark's house. It was addressed to Mr and Mrs Lewis and family, so Mum opened it and told them it was an invitation for them all to a 'Field Party' on the next Sunday afternoon.

'What's a field party?' asked Mark. 'Fields don't have birthdays.'

Dad and Mum remembered all the hard work everyone round there had done to make the new playing field. Dad had helped dig out the holes for the new climbing frames and swings, and Mum, Josie and Mark had been there all one Saturday morning when the bark was spread round the equipment. This was to make it safe and soft for children climbing and swinging and bouncing. There had been jumble sales, cake stalls, and sponsored walks and bike rides when everyone worked together to collect enough money to buy everything that was needed. Josie's class at school had drawn pictures and maps of how they wanted the playing field to look, and Mark's playgroup had helped to plant the new little trees around the field, one cold winter's day.

'This party is a thank-you one for everyone who helped to make the lovely new playing field,' said Mum. 'So we can all go.'

Josie had been to quite a lot of parties, and she liked wearing her pretty party dress, so she was surprised on Sunday when Mum told her and Mark to put on old clothes for the field party. But when they got there she was glad she didn't have to be careful all the time, because there were so many things to do.

The field looked great, with lots of flags and balloons tied to the equipment. There were two bouncy castles – one big one where the older children queued up for turns, and a smaller one for the younger children. There were lots of games, and some of them meant getting wet, but it was so warm that no one minded. Everyone sat around on rugs. There were books and toys, and Brian had brought his guitar. At tea-time everyone had a little bag of food, and there was plenty of squash.

After that they all got in a huge circle and did the hokey-cokey. Then Mum's friend Alison

carried something into the middle – it looked like a big white cake with one large candle on top. 'Our new playing field is one year old,' she said. 'Let's all sing happy birthday and blow out the candle!'

They did that – the wind helped too! Do you know – it wasn't a cake at all, but a big box, and inside there was a little present for each child.

There were lots of thank-yous – to all the people who had helped to make the field as well as the party.

'I like parties like that one,' said Mark. 'So many people having so much fun together.'

Story books

- Shirley Hughes, *Alfie Gives a Hand*, Picture Lions, 1985.
- Gill McLean, *Time to Get Up*, Tamarind, 1992.
- Tony Bradman, *Dilly's Birthday Party*, Mammoth, 1993.
- Pat Hutchins, *The Suprise Party*, Red Fox, 1993.
- Helen Oxenbury, *The Birthday Party*, Walker Books, 1988.

 ## Prayers

Sit round in a circle with reminders of the party in the centre. Say prayers of thanks for happy times. Remember those who never have a party, or never have enough to eat.

Note

It might be appropriate to use this theme when you expect new children to join your group. You could use it as a special way of welcoming them. It may be best not to use this to coincide with a particular child's birthday as it may seem like favouritism. It may fit in with a church/chapel anniversary or Saint's Day.

Hands and feet

Aim

To help children to think about how much they need their hands and feet and to appreciate all the things they can do with them, both for themselves and for other people.

29

Setting

Use one half of the room for the exploration of hands and the other half for feet. Cut out large and small hand and foot shapes to go on the wall in each area.

THINGS TO WEAR ON HANDS

- Pairs of gloves (rubber, plastic, gardening, workman's, motorcyclist's, golfer's, baby's, children's, adult's, disposable, mittens).

THINGS TO DO WITH HANDS

- Several washing-up bowls with small containers (e.g. bottle tops, scoops, small spoons, plastic straws, a doll's tea set) for water play.
- A further washing-up bowl, filled with bubbly water, with nail brushes.
- Towels for hand drying.
- Sticklebricks, Duplo and other bricks.
- Jigsaws, a shape sorter, bead threading.
- A keyboard.
- Pictures of people using their hands.

THINGS TO WEAR ON FEET

- Wellies, football boots, shoes, trainers, tap and ballet shoes, sandals, slippers, babies' shoes, men's large-size shoes and boots, ski boots, flippers, flip-flops.
- Socks, stockings and tights of different kinds.

THINGS TO DO WITH FEET

- Rope or tape to jump over, a balancing bar if possible, stepping stones (made from sides of cardboard boxes), cotton wool balls (for picking up with bare feet), a zebra crossing, large plastic boxes and baked bean tins to step on and off, home-made stilts made from empty tins, a climbing frame, a slide, soft balls for kicking.
- Pictures of people using their feet.
- Pictures of people in wheelchairs.

Sharing

What do we use our hands for? If we had only one hand, what would it be difficult to do? What do we use our feet for? How do you get about if you haven't got any feet? What's the most exciting thing you have ever done with your feet?

Play

Use the setting and everything in it.

Bible story
JOHN 13. 4–9

'Phew! It's hot, and it's been a jolly busy day,' said Matthew. The friends of Jesus (we call them the disciples) arrived back from all the places they had been to. They were tired, sticky and rather cross. They flopped down round the room and no one seemed to want to do anything.

It happened so long ago that there were no cars, or motorbikes, or buses to drive about in. Everyone walked everywhere on roads that were rough, stony and sandy. The people wore open sandals, so they all had very dusty feet.

Jesus came in and saw them all. What a lot of miserable faces there were! Everyone seemed to be waiting for someone else to do something. How could he change all that? Perhaps he could get them to begin to look after each other.

Very quietly and without any fuss, Jesus got a bowl of water and a towel. He began with James, who was sitting nearest the door. Jesus knelt down, took off James' sandals and washed the dust and dirt off his feet, then dried them with the towel. James said he felt much more comfortable now, and he thanked Jesus, who went on washing each person's feet.

At last he came to Peter, who had been watching what was happening. He had been so surprised that he couldn't say anything. Now with Jesus kneeling in front of him, ready to wash his feet, he said suddenly, 'Jesus, you are special. You shouldn't be doing this. We should be looking after you.'

Jesus said, 'You shouldn't just be looking after me, but looking after anyone who needs your help.'

That made everyone stop and think.

Activities

- Hand and finger painting.
- Foot printing (see Appendix).
- Preparing a salad or fruit salad.
- Make some bread dough using a ready-mix.
- Parachute/canopy games (see Appendix).
- Draw around hands and feet. Cut out and use as the base for collage work (e.g. decorating with fine pasta, small buttons, crushed egg-shell, coloured sand etc.).

Music and rhymes

SONGS

'I jump for joy as each new day dawns' (*BBP*)

'Two little eyes to look to God' (*JU* and *Junior Praise*)

'If you're happy and you know it, clap your hands' (*Apusskidu*)

'Stand up, clap hands, say thank you Lord' (add a 'foot' verse) (*Someone's Singing, Lord*)

RHYMES

Open your fingers
Now shut them tight.
Tuck them away till
They're out of sight.

Open your fingers
Now let them clap
Hold them up high
Then down in your lap.

Fling up your fingers
To reach the sky:
Flutter them down
And there let them lie.

HPPA

Point to the windows,
Point to the door.
Point to the ceiling,
Point to the floor.
Give a little shake,
Give a little clap,
Then put your hands behind your back.

Traditional

(*Vary, pointing to anything in the room, to catch the children out!*)

Big brown boots go
Tramp, tramp, tramp.
Little red shoes go
Stamp, stamp, stamp.
Silver slippers go
Trip, trip, trip.
And my two feet go
Skip, skip, skip.

Traditional

Drama and movement

- Play 'Simon says'.
- Do the 'Hokey Cokey' and other ring games.
- Use percussion instruments to encourage the children to make different kinds of movements with their hands and feet (e.g. loud drum-beats

for stamping, a rice shaker for small finger movements).

Another story

'Soon you'll be big enough to go to big school, Neil, because you're four years old.' Neil loved his playgroup very much and especially Mrs Parker, so he wasn't quite sure he wanted to leave playgroup and go to big school.

Then one morning, after he had come home from playgroup, Mum said, 'This afternoon we are going to see the school where you'll be going after the holidays and we'll meet Mrs Merrill, your new teacher.'

Neil wanted to know if Mrs Merrill would be like Mrs Parker, who was so good at playing games with him and the other children. Mum said, 'Mrs Merrill will be different, but I expect there are lots of things she is really good at.'

When they went into the classroom, Mrs Merrill was sitting by a table where some children were cutting and sticking and painting. She smiled at Mum and Neil and said how pleased she was to meet them, and she hoped they'd enjoy their afternoon in her classroom. So Mum and Neil sat down and watched what the children were doing. After a few minutes Neil began to play with the building bricks and looked at some of the books.

Then Mrs Merrill said it was nearly time to clear up all the activities, ready for song and story time. The children were only a bit bigger than Neil, but they were experts at clearing up, and soon all the bits of paper from off the floor were in the bin, and the glue had been wiped off the tables. The bricks were stacked in the brick box, the books were tidied up and Mrs Merrill never even had to get up from her chair.

Then the children sat round her on their chairs or on the carpet and they sang songs. Neil and Mum knew some of them, so they could both join in, but there were some new ones too. Mrs Merrill sang one that was quite funny. She told the children to listen carefully to see if she got it right: 'Baa baa green sheep, have you any milk?' Neil laughed so much that he nearly fell off his chair!

Then she told them all a story from Africa about Ijapa the tortoise. She held a little drum in her hand and her fingers tapped it lightly for the rain in the story, and then banged it quite hard for the thunder. It was great.

Neil said to his Mum, 'Mrs Merrill is different from Mrs Parker, and I think I'll like having her as my teacher. But why doesn't she get up and walk around the room?'

Mrs Merrill laughed when she heard Neil say that, and then Neil saw that her chair was a wheelchair. 'I can't use my feet,' said Mrs Merrill, 'so the children in my class do all the running about for me.'

Neil looked at her feet and then said, 'But your hands work really well, don't they!'

He decided he was going to like going to big school after all.

Story books

- Debbie Bailey, *Shoes*, Talkabout Books, Annick Press, 1991.
- Brian Wildsmith, *Whose Shoes?*, Oxford University Press, 1984.
- Georges Lemoine, *Hands, Feet and Paws*, Moonlight Publishing, 1991.
- Shirley Hughes, *Alfie's Feet*, Bodley Head, 1982.

 ## *Prayers*

Bring the hands and feet which were made during the activity session (or the hands and feet from the setting). Place them on the floor, with the children sitting round them. Ask the children to put their hands together for a 'thank-you' prayer for hands and the things we can do with them. Then all stand up, with feet wide apart, to thank God for the things we can do with our feet. Put feet together and pray for people who cannot use their feet. Hold hands in a circle, asking the children for the names of people who need their help. Pray for them and for each other.

Making it better

33

Setting

Turn the corners of the room into different areas:

HOSPITAL / CLINIC / DOCTOR'S SURGERY AREA

- Nurses' and doctors' outfits, a first-aid box, plasters, creams, bandages, slings, walking sticks, a telephone, a computer, pads of paper, pens, tissues, buckets, mops, cloths.

MENDING AREA

- Glue, staples, tapestry needles, buttons, a box for damaged toys, bits of Sellotape, pieces of fabric, damaged books, scissors, a hammer, nails, a screwdriver, screws (with an old table or bench), instant glue and glue remover, Copydex (for use only by adults), a dustpan and brush.

HOMELY COMFORT AREA

- A comfortable chair, cushions, soft toys, a rag doll.
- A grandparent figure or figure of trust.
- Books for looking at with an adult, a TV, a tape player (with a tape), a scrapbook of pictures of people the children know, tissues, pictures of people in caring situations.

Sharing

- What happens when you hurt yourself? Who helps you? How do they help?
- If you have broken something, where might you have to go for help?
- What makes you feel upset? (E.g. separation, arguments, being told off, 'it's not fair', someone dying, not feeling loved, feeling pushed out.) Who helps and how?
- If someone you know is upset, how can you help?

Play

Use the setting and everything in it for imaginative play.

Bible story

LUKE 18. 15–17

'Where's everybody, Mum?' asked Miriam as they walked home from school. Bethel was usually a very busy village, particularly when the children finished school and started off home. But today was different when they came out of school. It was really quiet, there weren't many grown-ups about at all.

Miriam's mother had come to fetch her, and she told her that lots of people were under the shady tree behind the synagogue (that's what the church in the village was called). The people were listening to Jesus. He was telling them wonderful stories about how God loved them all. Of course, some of the children wanted to be there, and they raced off down the village street. When they got to the place where everyone was gathered together, two people stopped them and said, 'Go away and play. Children can't come here. They make too much noise. Jesus mustn't be disturbed.

'We'll be ever so quiet,' said Samuel.

'Yes,' the others said, 'you'll hardly notice us at all.'

The two people who had stopped them thought hard. 'All right, you can stay here, but don't let us hear a sound from you, or off you'll go at once!'

A few children decided to go home, but Samuel and Miram, with their friends Isaac and Naomi, sat down where they were so they could listen. They couldn't hear very well, so gradually they wriggled a bit nearer and nearer to Jesus. Then he told everyone a story about a man building a house on sand. That made the children laugh – it was such a silly idea. Everyone turned to look at them and said, 'Shhh!' and the two people who'd been rather cross started to come over towards them.

But Jesus finished his story and stood up. 'Please don't send the children away,' he said. 'Let them come here, so that we can all see them.' He lifted Isaac and Naomi on to his knees and put his arms round Miriam and Samuel's shoulders. He told everyone how special children are and how important it is

 to be sure that they are loved and that they are safe and cared for. 'Sit down here near me,' he said, 'and I'll tell a story that you'll really like.' And he did.

Activities

- Provide large sheets of coloured paper, large brushes (sizes 10, 12 and 16), and pots of thick powder paint (use ready-mix paint or experiment

with mixing powder paint and water to a similar consistency, adding a drop of washing-up liquid to each jar).

- Provide suitable covering for tables and floor, and old shirts for the children. Encourage them to paint freely.

- Make some simple home-made books with pictures of people cut or torn by the chiildren from magazines.

 **Music and rhymes**

SONGS

'Four friends carry a neighbour' (*BBP*)

'I'm sitting by myself' (*BBP*)

'When I'm feeling down and sad' (*BBP*)

'Jesus' hands were kind hands' (*Junior Praise*)

'Singing Lord' (*Junior Praise*)

Poor Mary sits a-weeping
A-weeping, a-weeping a-weeping
Poor Mary sits a-weeping
On a bright summer's day.

Traditional

(*Change the verses as appropriate.*)

'Miss Polly had a dolly' (*Apusskidu*)

'Humpty, Dumpty sat on a wall'

'Jack and Jill went up the hill'

'In a cottage in a wood' (*Apusskidu*)

 **Drama and movement**

Half the children sing 'Ring-a-ring o'roses'. When they fall down the other children, playing the part of ambulances and paramedics, zoom in to pick everybody up. Take it in turns!

Another story

'It's playtime, children,' said Mrs Lees. 'I'm afraid you can't have the big climbing frames out on the grass today because it is still wet.' Mrs Lees said they could have all the bikes and trucks and wheeled toys out on the tarmac. 'Do you all remember about taking turns on them?' she asked.

'Yes,' said the children.

Aduke and Bola did too. They often played together and shared toys quite happily. They both especially liked the big blue tractor with the trailer behind, because one could drive and the other could ride in the back and then they could swop over.

Today, as soon as the door was opened, they raced out and arrived at the tractor almost exactly together. 'Me first to drive,' said Aduke, 'and then you.'

'No,' said Bola. 'Me first and then you.'

They started shouting at each other, getting louder and louder and getting quite cross too. I'm not sure who pushed the other one first, but before long they had both fallen down and were crying. Aduke had a bump on her knee and Bola had hurt her hand.

Mrs Lees came up to see what was happening. Neither of them stopped crying, so she picked them both up and gave them a hug, one on each side of her. 'I think a bit of making it better is needed,' she said. 'How about going into the bathroom and getting some tissues to wipe your faces and where you have hurt yourselves, and then we can see what needs to be done.'

She took them inside and found the box of tissues and went to get the First Aid box from the cupboard. When she came back a minute later they were using the tissues to dry each other's tears. Aduke washed Bola's hand very carefully, and Bola gently wiped the mud off Aduke's knee. The bumped places were red and sore, but there were no cuts and no blood.

Mrs Lees' jar of cream from the First Aid box had a lovely smell. They dipped their fingers into the cream and smoothed some on each other's poorly places. There was even enough left over for the tiny red mark on Mrs Lees' wrist.

'You two are good at making things better now,' said Mrs Lees. 'How about going to play at being nurses in the hospital corner?'

Aduke and Bola had a lovely time there and they forgot all about the fight over the big blue tractor and trailer.

Do you think they'll remember to take turns properly next time?

Story books

- Shirley Hughes, *Alfie Gives a Hand*, Picture Lions, 1985.
- Jean and Gareth Anderson, *Topsy and Tim Go Fishing*, Blackie, 1963.
- Diana Noonan, *The Best Loved Bear*, Picture Hippo, 1994.
- Shirley Hughes, *Alfie Gets in First*, Bodley Head, 1981.

Prayer

Lay two giant hands (cut from large sheets of coloured paper) in the centre of the floor. Ask the children to take from the setting items which remind them of ways in which people help them to feel better and ways in which they can help others. Place them on the hands and use them as the focus for a 'Thank you for making it better' prayer.

Note

Be aware that this topic may raise issues relating to the safeguarding of children from various forms of abuse. If this happens, you will need to follow the procedures which have been adopted by your church or organisation.

Losing and finding

Setting

- Create hiding places within your room using boxes, drapes over tables and chairs, a playtunnel, a playbarrel etc.
- Set up a treasure hunt within the setting. Hide in advance some small objects (e.g. pasta shells, conkers, shiny buttons, bottle tops, shells, stones).
- Have a selection of nesting dolls, pots, baskets and containers with small objects hidden in them.
- Provide tissue, crepe paper, small pieces of fabric, and small objects for making hidden presents.
- Provide some toy woolly sheep [P]

Sharing

Have you ever lost something? What was it? Did you find it? Where did you find it? Who helped you to find it?

Play

Play 'Hunt the treasure', providing a large container into which the children place the things they find (do it this way to avoid being competitive). If you are using anything edible, make sure that it is distributed fairly later in the session.

Bible story

Luke 15. 4–6: The story of the lost sheep

. . . 97, 98, 99. There was one missing! Jacob was horrified. Which one was it? Was it Blackears, or Nosey, or Silly Skipper, or Patch? Was it Wandering Woolly? That's who it was. Jacob might have guessed.

It was getting dark. Jacob had brought all the sheep up the hill to the cave, where they would be safe for the night. Safe from the wolves who prowled the hills at dead of night.

There was only one thing for it. Jacob must go back down the hill, searching everywhere for Wandering Woolly.

He left the other sheep safely in the cave and set off back the way they had come. Down the hill he went searching, behind rocks, under bushes, in thickets and by a little stream. Every so often he stopped to listen. Could he hear a sad little 'baaa'? He couldn't hear anything except the sounds of the night. He called, 'Woolly, Woolly!' but there was no reply.

At the side of the path were some very high, steep rocks. He climbed to the top and saw an even higher one in front of him. Once more he called, 'Woolly, Woolly!' This time he heard a tiny sound. Was it a bleat? Was it Woolly? He climbed further. He called again. This time he knew he heard a bleat. Round the corner of the rock he climbed, and there, through the darkness he could see a faint white shape. It was Woolly, stuck on the rock, but waving his tail in excitement. He was so pleased to be found!

Very carefully Jacob helped him down from the rock. Woolly was so tired that Jacob put him on his shoulders and carried him all the way up the hill to safety, and to all his brothers and sisters.

Jacob was tired, but so happy: . . . 97, 98, 99, 100. All there. All safe. Time to go to sleep.

Activities

- Play 'Kim's game' at a very simple level, helping the children to remember as a group.

- Play 'Hide and Seek'.
- Hide some tiny chocolate eggs, either around your outside area (if it and the weather are suitable) or in the room in which you meet.

Music and rhymes

Songs

'We tend our sheep' (omit last verse) (*BBP*)

'The Lord is my Shepherd, I'll follow him alway' (*Sound of Living Waters*)

'Three little kittens'

'O where, O where has may little dog gone?'

Rhymes

Jenny Muddlecombe has lost her hat
She can't find it anywhere, well fancy that.
She walked down the High Street and
everyone said,
'Funny Jenny Muddlecombe,
Her hat is on her head.'

HPPA

Five little ducks went out one day
Over the hills and far away.
Mother duck said, 'Quack, quack, quack,
quack.'
Four little ducks came swimming back.

Four little ducks ...
Three little ducks ...
Two little ducks ...
One little duck ...

Mother Duck went out one day
Over the hills and far away.
Mother Duck said, 'Quack, quack, quack,
quack.'
And five little ducks came swimming back.

Traditional

Tommy Thumb, Tommy Thumb, (*thumb hidden*)
Where are you?
Here I am, Here I am, (*show thumb*)
How do you do.

Traditional

(*Use names for the other fingers: Peter Pointer (first finger), Johnny Long (middle), Ruby Ring (fourth), Baby Small, Fingers All.*)

What's the matter, what's the matter?
There is such a fuss.
Everyone is rushing.
Have they missed the bus?

Is there something broken?
Has someone bumped their knees?
Can we smell a pan burnt dry?
No! Dad has lost his keys.

Drama and movement

Use the whole room. Encourage the children to make themselves as small as possible, hiding so that they cannot be seen. On the clap of a hand ask them to spring in the air, so that thay can all be seen. Repeat, encouraging the children to curl into different shapes. Act out the story of the lost sheep. One child can be the shepherd, followed by the others being the sheep. Choose one child to 'go missing' somewhere in the room. When the shepherd has found the lost sheep, change roles.

Story

Ask an adult to tell the children in an exciting way about a time when they lost something (e.g. keys). (Note: Do not use a story about a lost child.)

Story books

Eric Hill, *Where's Spot?*, Heinemann, 1985.

Nick Butterworth and Mick Inkpen, *Ten Silver Coins*, Marshall Pickering, 1989.

Mick Inkpen, *Nothing*, Hodder Children's Books, 1996.

Shirley Hughes, *Hiding*, Walker Books, 1995.

Prayers

Put in the centre of the group toy woolly lambs and some nesting toys. Say thank you to Jesus that he is always with us, especially when we are lost or lonely or sad or frightened.

Preparation

Draw patterns with a white candle on sheets of paper. Make watery paint.

Pack a parcel.

Ask in advance for adults and children to bring toy woolly sheep.

Note

Sensitivity will be needed when using this theme.

Eggs

Aim

To help the children to develop a sense of wonder at the miracle of new life and thank God for it.

Setting

- If possible, an incubator with eggs in it and/or a chicken hutch with chicks.
- Straw in a box with an uneven number of eggs. (Hens will not sit on an even number of eggs because they cannot move them around easily.)
- Eggs – chicken, duck, bantam, quail, goose, ostrich, as available.
- An old empty nest (never raid one!). A local museum may be able to lend you an exhibit.
- Hard-boiled eggs, a fresh egg (cracked open), a fried egg on toast, scrambled egg on toast, boiled egg with 'soldiers' (bread-and-butter fingers), meringues.
- An egg separator.
- Easter eggs, decorated cardboard eggs, small chocolate eggs, onyx eggs, wooden eggs, painted eggs, soapstone eggs.
- An egg tree, with manufactured eggs.
- A variety of egg cups.
- Egg cosies, a teapot cosy shaped like a hen.
- An egg crock.
- Egg boxes.

Sharing

What kind of eggs do you like to eat? Where do eggs come from (e.g. hens, birds, snakes, crocodiles, turtles, dinosaurs)? What are the different ways they can be cooked (e.g. boiled, scrambled, fried, omlettes, meringues, etc.).

Play

Investigate, touch and taste the things in the setting.

Bible story

MATTHEW 23. 37

Jesus and his friends, the disciples, had had a long walk from Galilee to the big city of Jerusalem. The last part was up quite a high hill, but they knew that when they got to the top they would be able to see the houses down in Jerusalem, with the high wall all round them and with the Temple in the middle. The Temple was a very special big church. They stopped to look at this view and to have a short rest before going down into the city to find where they were going to stay.

'Just think of all the people down there and how they live and what they do,' said James. 'There will be happy people there and sad people. Some who work hard and who are kind to each other, and some who aren't. I wonder what happens to them all.'

Jesus told them about when he had visited Jerusalem with his parents when he was a boy. 'We slept down there near the city wall,' he said. 'One morning quite early, I woke up before my mother and father. I went out and sat on the grass. It was so quiet, I could hear the birds singing, and then I heard the cluck-cluck sound that a hen makes, coming nearer and nearer. She came past where I was sitting, leading her little chicks. I think there were about eight of them. They made quite a noise, all cheeping together and scratching at the ground to find little bits to eat. It was fun watching them scurry round and seeing how worried the mother hen got when they wandered off. At last she seemed to call them all back, and then she sat down on the ground and spread her wings out. The chicks all crawled under her feathers, where she had kept them warm when they were in their eggs. If a little head popped out she tucked it back in again with her beak. They were all safe.'

'Why are you telling us this?' asked Thomas.

Jesus replied, 'I wish Jerusalem could be like a mother hen and that all the people could be safe inside the city, like little chicks under the hen's wings. But I'm afraid it can't be like that.' He sat quite still and looked very sad. Jesus knew it was going to be very difficult for a lot of people in Jerusalem quite soon, and for him and his friends too.

Activities

● Have an egg-and-spoon race with hard-boiled eggs.

● Make some egg and mayonnaise sandwiches.

● Make some meringues, if possible using a microwave to get them done in a short time (see Appendix).

● Provide some good-sized pieces of egg-shaped paper for decoration with yellow, brown and white collage materials including beads, lace and feathers.

● Provide some egg-shaped paper for painting.

● Use dried, crumpled egg-shells, dyed with food colouring, as collage materials to decorate small egg-shaped cards. Hang them on a branch to make an egg tree.

● Make biscuits using egg and chicken-shaped cutters.

Music and rhymes

SONGS

'Happy Easter we will say' (*BBP*)

'Chick, chick, chick, chicken' (*Traditional*)

'There once was an ugly duckling' (*Words/music Frank Loesser, from MGM film* Hans Christian Andersen)

'Alleluia, alleluia, winter has fled' (*BBP*)
Add this new verse:
Alleluia, alleluia,
Out of the eggs come the baby chickens.
Alleluia, alleluia,
Jesus is risen and he's here.

'Have you seen the pussy cat sitting on the wall?' (*Junior Praise*)
Sing this chorus with these new verses:

Have you seen the fluffy goose sitting on her nest,
Have you heard her qua-a-arking noise?
Have you seen the brown hen sitting on her nest,
Have you heard her clucking sound?

Have you seen the children searching for the eggs,
Have you heard them calling out?
Have you seen the adults watching them have fun,
Have you heard them say 'Well done'?

RHYMES

Five little Easter eggs lovely colours wore.
Daddy ate the red one, and then there were four.
Four little Easter eggs, two and two you see.
Mummy ate the orange one and then there were three.
Three little Easter eggs – before I knew
My brother ate the yellow one; then there were two.
Two little Easter eggs – oh what fun!
My sister ate the green one, and then there was one.
One little Easter egg – see me run.
I ate the blue one. Now there are none.

Word Play, Finger Play

Drama and movement

- Pretend to be unhatched chicks, curled up within their eggs. Peck the shells to make a hole. Gradually break out. Fluff out feathers and wings. Begin to scuttle around, scurrying into a group for shelter under the wings of the mother hen.
- Sing and act out 'The Birdie Song'.

Another story

Linda and Mark were helping Mum take down the Christmas tree. They packed away all the decorations, ready for next year. The children had really loved the tree with its bright shiny balls and twinkling lights

It's going to be a long time to wait until next Christmas,' said Linda. 'Can we have trees for other times, like birthdays?'

Mum remembered seeing a picture in a magazine. 'I think it was an Easter tree,' she said. 'Let's see if we can find out about it, then we might be able to make our own.'

A few weeks later, Mum brought home a little branch that she had found lying on the ground. It had no leaves on and looked rather bare, so the children were surprised when she said it could be their Easter tree.

'First of all, we'll paint it,' Mum explained. 'Then we'll find something to stand it in while we think about how to decorate it.' They spread newspapers all over the table and painted the branch white. It was a bit difficult and rather messy, but the branch looked better already. Dad found something to stand it in so that it was firm and wouldn't fall over.

'We have eggs at Easter time,' said Mark. 'But I don't think we could hang them on the branch – not real eggs.'

Linda said, 'We could draw pictures of eggs and cut them out to hang up.' So the table was covered with newspapers again and Mum cut lots of egg shapes out of card for Linda and Mark to paint and decorate. They glued on bits of shiny paper and ribbon and sequins. Mum threaded cotton through each egg shape, and then they hung them on the bare branch to make their Easter tree. It looked lovely.

'Let's tell all our friends about our Easter tree,' said the children, 'then they could make them as well.' Perhaps you would like to have a go too.

Story books

- Caryll Houselander and Tomie de Paola, *Petook*, Burns & Oates, 1990.
- René Mettler, *The Egg*, Moonlight Publishing/First Discovery, 1990.
- William Mayne, *The Mouse and the Egg*, Lion, 1995.
- Suzie Jane Tanner, *An Egg*, Lion, 1990.

Prayers

Gather in a circle round a central low table. Place on the table a small flower pot filled with moss or crushed green tissue paper for each child, and a basket of fresh eggs (hard-boiled if you think it advisable!). Invite the children carefully to take an egg from the basket and rejoin the circle. Then ask them to close their eyes and gently feel the smoothness and shape of the eggs. Thank God for eggs to eat and eggs which hatch into new life. Ask the children to place their eggs in the flower pots, then to sing 'Thank you for the world so sweet'. (Provide small plastic bags for the children to take their eggs home.)

Note

This theme is particularly suitable for Easter, but can be adapted for use at other times.

The supermarket

Aim

To help the children to appreciate that ordinary things can be very special

Setting

Lay out chairs in one part of the room to look like the narrow aisles of a supermarket, using the seats of the chairs as shelves.

STOCK

Packets, tins, plastic bottles, fruit and vegetables (plastic if possible).

THE CHECKOUT

A till, money (1p and 2p pieces), toy paper money.

SHOPPING CONTAINERS

Carrier bags, baskets, a child's trolley or baby walker, a trolley on wheels, small cardboard boxes, handbags and purses (with plastic cards and money).

Sharing

Where do you do your shopping? Who do you go to the supermarket with? What do you like most about shopping? What do you do to help? What is bought that you like to eat? What is bought that you like to drink?

Play

Use the setting for creative play.

Bible story
LUKE 22. 7–15

'We are going to have the special meal tonight,' said Jesus to his friends one Thursday in Jerusalem, 'and we're going to have to get it ready.'

Peter and John rushed off to the market to get the food. John said, 'That stall near the entrance to the market is really good for fresh

meat, so we can get what we need for the lamb stew there.'

'Yes,' said Peter, 'and at the stall next door we can get the eggs and the salt.'

'What about the dates and herbs? Where's the best place for them?' asked John.

They walked through the market, keeping a good look-out for what they wanted, and they were lucky because Peter spotted a little stall in a shady archway, with juicy fat dates and bright green herbs.

Soon the two men were quite laden down with all the baskets of food they'd bought. Suddenly one of them stopped. 'We've nearly forgotten the two most important things for our meal – the bread and the wine. What a good thing we remembered in time!'

It was a good thing too, because at the supper that night, Jesus explained to them all that bread and wine would always be remembered at meals like this one, to help people understand him and how much he would love and care for every person in the world for ever.

That meal happened a long, long time ago, but what Jesus said then is still remembered every time there is a special meal of bread and wine for Christian people. It is usually called the Lord's Supper or Holy Communion. It's very special.

Activities

- Look at a picture of the Last Supper and talk about it.

- Provide modelling dough for the children to make model food (see Appendix).
- Build a pyramid with tins.
- Provide a large supermarket trolley made from strong paper [P]. Fill the outline of the trolley with pictures of food cut from catalogues and supplements [P].

 **Music and rhymes**

SONGS

'I like eating' (*BBP, FG* and *JU*)

'From hand to hand' (*BBP*)

A little girl went walking,
She walked into a store,
She bought a pound of sausages
And laid them on the floor.
The girl began to whistle,
She whistled up a tune,
And all the little sausages
Danced around the room.

HPPA

(*Sing to the tune of 'I had a little nut tree'.*)

RHYMES

Five sticky buns in the baker's shop,
Big and brown with sugar on the top.
(Name) came along with a penny to pay,
Paid one penny and took a bun away.

Four sticky buns . . .

Three sticky buns . . .

Two sticky buns . . .

One sticky bun . . .

No sticky buns in a baker's shop,
Big and brown with sugar on the top.
(Name) came along with a penny to pay.
'Sorry,' said the baker, 'we have no buns left today.'

Traditional

 **Drama and movement**

Miming and guessing: pushing a trolley, stacking the shelves, showing a customer where something is, stretching up to the top shelf, packing the shopping, being a security guard, someone with a charity tin.

Another story

'Do I have to come?' Roger was fed up. He didn't like going to the supermarket. When he was little he could sit in the trolley as Mum and Dad pushed it round, and he could see all the things on the shelves. Sometimes he could reach out and choose the packet of biscuits or cereals he liked.

Now Roger was too big to sit in the trolley seat, and he had to walk round the supermarket. He could only see the bottom shelves, and there never seemed to be the things he liked on there. I expect you can guess how he grumbled and walked slowly behind Mum and Dad's trolley, so no one enjoyed the trip to the supermarket very much.

Then one day Dad had a good idea. 'Why doesn't Roger have a supermarket trolley of his own to push round?' he said. 'One that is just the right size for him.'

Mum said she'd seen one at the Nearly New Shop [or a similar name as appropriate], and she'd get it in time for the next shopping trip.

Everything went really well. Roger pushed his own trolley round the supermarket, and he found a jar of his favourite honey on one shelf and some of the crisps he really liked on another, so they went into his trolley. He didn't grumble or walk slowly. In fact, he went a bit too fast round the corner of one big block of shelves, and his trolley knocked into a huge stack of tins of soup that were piled up like a pyramid. One of the tins on the edge slipped on to the floor, then there was a great clattering noise as all the tins fell down and rolled all over the place.

Roger stood still and began to cry. The noise had frightened him and he thought everyone would be very cross. But instead people began to laugh, and one of the shop-keepers came running up. He laughed too. 'Don't worry,' he said to Roger. 'Just be glad it wasn't eggs!'

Story books

- Jean and Gareth Anderson, *Topsy and Tim Go Shopping*, Blackie, 1980.
- Susie Lacome, *At the Shops*, Walker, 1993.
- Margaret Gordon, *The Supermarket Mice*, Picture Puffin, 1986.
- PPA, *Let's Go Shopping*, Young World Publications, 1972.

Prayers

Ask the children to sit in a circle with a basket of small bread rolls in the centre. Pass one roll slowly round the circle while you sing 'From hand to hand' (*BBP*). Then ask the children to help themselves and to take one home.

The garden centre

Aim

To help children discover how plants grow and to thank God for them.

Setting

- A garden umbrella, table and chairs.
- Large plants/trees.
- Safe tools, a watering can, a wheelbarrow (full size).
- Plant pots (mixed sizes), plant trays, bulb fibre (in bags), compost, pebbles, gravel, etc.
- Plant pots planted with attractive weeds (e.g. daisies, groundsel, tree seedlings).
- Plant pots planted with silk flowers.
- Packets of seeds, beans, peas etc.
- Posters and catalogues.
- A shopping trolley with boxes, a baby walker, baskets.
- Rubber gloves, aprons.
- A toy till and toy money.

Sharing

Who has been to a garden centre? How did you get there? Why did you go? What did you see? What colours were the things you saw? What did you smell?

Play

Use the setting and everything in it for imaginative play.

Bible story

JOHN 20. 10–18

It was a lovely morning. The sun was shining and the sky was blue. But Mary was very sad.

Her best friend had died. She decided to go for a walk in the garden she loved. It was a garden which was full of lovely trees and plants. Some of the plants, called herbs, had very special smells. Mary loved touching them with her fingers and then smelling her hand. Sometimes her skirt would brush against them and the perfume would stay on the material for a long time.

The garden also had small caves in the rocks, and it was in one of these that her friend's body had been laid. She went to the garden to be quiet and to say her final goodbyes to her friend Jesus. There were geraniums and hibiscus in bloom, and bougainvillaeas trailing over the rocks.

Mary reached the cave. 'What happened? Where is Jesus?' she cried. The big stone that covered the doorway was rolled away and the cave was empty. She burst into tears. 'What have they done with him?' she called as she ran back through the garden.

She rounded a corner and bumped into a man. 'Whatever is the matter?' he said.

'They've taken Jesus away, and I don't know what they have done with him,' she answered.

'Mary,' said the man.

Mary looked up, opened her eyes wide and said 'Jesus!' (She had recognised his voice.) 'Jesus, you are alive!'

'Shhh!' he said. 'Don't tell everyone.'

'Can I tell Peter and John?' she asked.

'Yes, you can – I will see them later.'

Mary was so excited. Her feet ran so fast as she rushed home to tell the others, 'Jesus is alive!'

Activities

- Make an Easter garden (see Appendix).
- Plant seeds and bulbs, plant out young plants, arrange flowers.

- Make seed packets by sticking pictures from seed catalogues on to envelopes. Put sunflower seeds, grass seeds, pips etc. inside.
- Plant mustard and cress seeds on damp tissue or in egg-shells filled with soil.
- Play 'Snap' and other matching games with cards made from flower pictures and catalogues [P].
- Make a poster with cut-out flower pictures.
- Visit a nearby private garden or church garden.

Music and rhymes

SONGS

'Just a tiny seed' (*BBP*)

'Here we go round the mulberry bush'

'Down came the raindrops' (Minnie R. Boyd, in *Child Songs*)

'All things bright and beautiful'

RHYMES

I had a little cherry stone
I put it in the ground
And when next year I came to look
A tiny shoot I found.
The shoot grew upwards day by day
And then became a tree.
I picked the rosy cherries
And ate them for my tea.

HPPA

Drama and movement

Act out a visit to a garden centre.

Another story

'I do wish we had a garden,' said Sally. 'I love flowers and would love to grow some of my own.' Steve and Sally lived in a flat, so they didn't have a garden to play in where they could dig in the soil and sit on the grass.

'Aunty Kath has a lovely garden,' said Steve.

'Yes, I know,' said Sally. 'Do you remember what I did there last time we went? I picked the daisies and buttercups on the lawn and made little flower arrangements in the tiny jars and doll-size cups and jugs that Aunty Kath found me.'

'I think we are going again soon.'

The next week they did, and Sally picked more daisies and buttercups for her little pots.

Steve was not so interested in the flowers – he went off to see where Uncle Jack was working in the vegetable part of the garden. Perhaps he'd be digging the soil ready to plant out the little green seedlings that would grown into cabbages one day, or he'd be pulling up the weeds in the rows of carrots and beans. Then Steve would put on his boots to help him. Best of all though, was going to inspect the onions, and particularly one special onion that Uncle Jack was growing for a competition called 'The biggest onion in town'. Steve was sure this would be the winner because it was huge and seemed bigger every time they looked at it.

'I'd like to grow things for a competition,' said Steve. 'But we haven't got a garden at our flat.'

Uncle Jack thought carefully, then he said, 'Next year in the spring, I'll give you a special seed you can plant in a pot. You'll have to water it and give it some plant food, then if it grows well you can enter it for 'The tallest sunflower in town' competition.

Sally wanted to join in too, and Aunty Kath said she could enter the competition for 'The smallest flower arrangement in town' because she was so good with the tiny flowers and leaves in the little jars.

When competition time came round next year, Steve had a sunflower that was taller than him, Sally had a pretty little flower arrangement in a thimble, and, of course, Uncle Jack had another huge onion that he had grown.

I don't know if they were the winners, but I do know they had lots of fun.

Story books

- Hepplethwaite and Kavanagh, *Our Two Gardens*, Hunt and Thorpe, 1991.
- Philip Parker, *Sunflowers*, Picture Puffin Fact Book, 1990.

Prayers

Put a green cloth on the table. Arrange the tray gardens and some plants to make an attractive display. Have a basket of leaves from different kinds of trees. Encourage each child to choose a leaf and to look at it carefully. Ask what names of plants and flowers the children know. Say a prayer of thanks for all the flowers, plants and trees in God's creation.

Preparation

- Try to visit your local garden centre for ideas and resources.
- Make 'Snap' cards and other matching games from flower pictures in catalogues.

Note

- Some children will not have had the experience of having a garden or visiting a garden centre. Sensitivity is needed.
- This theme is particularly suitable for Easter.

Mini-beasts

Setting

THE ROOM

- Put up pictures and posters around the walls showing small creatures of all kinds around the walls. Make or use mobiles of small creatures.

WOODY AREA

- Put some cloth or brown paper on the floor. Arrange on it tree branches, shrubbery material, tree bark, rotten wood etc. Make a cobweb with thread and fasten it in the tree.

SOIL AND STONE AREA

- Place a large tray on the floor (which has been protected).
- Put a mound of soil onto the tray. Add stones and earwigs, millipedes, woodlice and beetles (real or imitation).
- Add terracotta flower pots and snails.

OBSERVATORY

- Use sweet jars (with holes in their lids) to display a wormery, stick insects on privet and caterpillars on appropriate leaves.
- Use a screw-top jar (essential) for spider's eggs.
- Display a wasps' nest and a honeycomb.

PROVIDE

- Magnifying glasses, insect viewers, old spoons, ice-lolly sticks and books about mini-beasts.

Sharing

Look at the mini-beasts together. Ask the children if they know what the creatures are called. Where are they usually found? How do they move? Why are they so small?

Listen to the mini-beasts. Talk about the noises they make. Which are your favourite ones?

Play

Use the magnifying glasses and insect viewers to look at the mini-beasts. Use the lolly sticks and old spoons to explore the soil carefully, making sure the creatures are not harmed. Place the snails and the flower pots on a large sheet of matt paper (e.g. sugar paper), and watch them make trails. Let the children feel the tickle of the spider on their skin and a caterpillar creeping across their hands. Listen to a snail eating a lettuce leaf and a wood-louse moving on a piece of card.

Bible story

JUDGES 14. 8

BZZZZ . . . BZZZZ . . . bzzzz . . . bzzzz . . . bzzzz . . . bzzzz. The old queen bee was getting tired, but she knew she had to find a good place for a new nest for her worker bees before she died.

It had to be in exactly the right place, away from the old nest, near plenty of flowers so the bees could collect pollen, and in a quiet place so the bees wouldn't be disturbed by people walking and talking nearby. It had to be safe too, as there are birds and animals that attack bees' nests. Perhaps an old tree or a cave would do.

The queen bee set out, followed by a long trail of worker bees. She zoomed up in circles, getting higher and higher all the time, looking for the right place. Ah, that hole in that tree down there looks good, but there's a bird there already, building a nest. How about that cave? No, there's a family of bats living there. Suddenly the queen bee spotted something gleaming white down there among the flowers. There weren't any people around either. She circled lower and lower, with the hundreds of bees following her every move.

The whiteness she had seen from up high turned out to be the bones of a big animal that had died quite a long time ago. They were so clean and seemed to be waiting to be used, and the queen bee found lots of useful corners. She led her cloud of worker bees in to take over their new home. She could rest now. As she settled down, the queen bee thought to herself, I wonder if this animal liked honey? It was probably a lion. Do lions like honey?

 ## Activities

- Provide small pieces of paper, small pots of paint (e.g. in individual-portion jam jars) and tiny brushes (e.g. nail-varnish brushes) for the children to paint tiny pictures of mini-beasts.
- Fold a piece of sugar paper in half. Provide thick paint and large brushes. Encourage the children to put blobs of paint on one side of the paper. Fold the paper over and press firmly. Open it up to see the pattern – which may resemble butterflies!
- Create nooks and crannies using large cardboard boxes, blankets over tables etc. Hide in them.
- Go outside, if possible visiting someone's garden, on a search for mini-beasts: lifting stones (and putting them back carefully), looking at the backs of leaves and pieces of dead wood, turning over the soil, investigating a compost heap, looking for greenfly, blackfly etc.

 ## Music and rhymes

SONGS

'I love the pit, pit, patter of the raindrops' (*BBP*)

'God made furry things' (*BBP*)

'All things bright and beautiful'

Thank you, Lord, for mini-beasts, (x 3)
Right where they are.

Thank you, Lord, for wiggly worms, (x 3)
Right where they are.

Thank you, Lord, for buzzing bees, (x 3)
Right where they are.

Thank you, Lord, for slimy snails, (x 3)
Right where they are.

Thank you, Lord, for spinning spiders, (x 3)
Right where they are.

Junior Praise, adapted

(*To the tune of 'Thank you Lord for this fine day'.*)

RHYMES

'Incy wincy spider'

'Little Arabella Miller' (*Traditional*)

Frogs jump,
Caterpillars hump,
Worms wiggle,
Bugs jiggle,
But I walk.

HPPA

Big black spider,
Climbing up the wall,
Never, never, never
Seems to fall.
Yet I always fall
When I climb the gate.
I've only got two legs
And he's got eight.

HPPA

I wish I was a little grub
With whiskers on my tummy,
I'd climb into the honey pot
And make my tummy gummy.
And then I'd crawl all over you
And make your tummy gummy too.

Drama

Act out being:

- stick insects (still and then jerky)
- scurrying ants
- slithering worms
- slow snails
- spiders (long legs)
- bees and flies zooming and hovering.

Accompany this with homemade instruments:

- yoghurt pots covered in clingfilm for finger tapping
- plastic containers filled with soil, sand and rice to make slithery and tiny-feet sounds.

Another story

'Hello, Yvonne, what are you doing here?' said Mrs Banks, who was in the kitchen at the church. She was arranging some flowers in a vase to go on the table at the front of the church. They were bright yellow chrysanthemums that had glossy dark-green leaves. The brass vase had been polished so you could see your face in it. Mrs Banks couldn't, as she was too tall, but Yvonne could. Yvonne was seven years old. Her mother kept the church clean and tidy and Yvonne often helped her. She liked polishing the brass vase particularly. Yvonne was in the kitchen watching Mrs Banks because she liked to smile at herself in the bright shiny brass vase. It was like a mirror, except that it made her face go a funny shape.

Suddenly she saw something else moving in the mirror. 'Oh, what's that?' she said. She looked very carefully. It was a small snail going slowly up a flower stalk towards a bright yellow bud. What a surprise for Yvonne and Mrs Banks, and for the snail!

'It must have come a long way from the garden where these flowers were picked,' said Mrs Banks. 'Probably in a van, then at the flower shop and now here at our church. What shall we do with it?'

'Let's take it into church and then put it outside on some grass and leaves afterwards,' said Yvonne. The snail had come out of its shell again and was waving its little feelers as if to say yes. Together they went into the church. Mrs Banks carried the flowers carefully and Yvonne made sure the doors were open and that no one knocked into them.

It was Yvonne's turn that morning to choose a special hymn that the children knew. Can you guess what she chose? 'All things bright and beautiful, all creatures great and small.' Yvonne and Mrs Banks smiled at each other when they sang the word 'small'. It was their secret snail they were singing about, and they knew they would make sure he was back in the grass outside again after his great adventure. After all, the snail had come a long way to come to church.

Story books

- Eric Carle, *The Very Hungry Caterpillar*, Picture Puffin, 1974.
- Pat Wynne Jones, *The Tale of Twinette the Spider*, Lion, 1972.
- David Pelham, *Sam's Sandwich*, Random House, 1990.
- Babette Cole and Ron Van Der Meer, *Bible Beasties*, HarperCollins, 1993.

Prayers

Put pictures the children have painted and/or some of the containers with minibeasts in the middle of the group. Ask the children to curl up very small. Thank God for small creatures, for their different shapes and colours, for the busy things they do and the useful things they do for us.

Preparation

You'll need all the help you can get, so don't be afraid to ask other people. Try to overcome any fears you have of small creatures and share with the children the wonder of their creation.

You may decide that the whole session would work well in someone's garden, if one is available – and if the weather is all right.

Water is precious

Aim

To help children to think about water — where it can be found, and how essential it is for life.

Setting

- Play a tape of water sounds [P].

POND AREA

- Baby baths and large washing-up bowls filled with water and pond life (water cress quickly roots). Surround with pot plants.
- An aquarium tank or a deep container for fish.

WEATHER AREA

- Umbrellas, welly boots, kagools, anoraks, foil puddles.
- Hang artificial rain from the ceiling (see Appendix) [P].

SEA AREA

- Place blue and yellow fabric on the floor to represent sea and sand. On the blue fabric place toy boats, a li-lo, an inner tube etc. On the yellow fabric place bucket and spade, a deck chair, sea shells, a swimming costume, a beach ball etc.

GROWING AREA

- Saucers, jam jars, a hyacinth jar.
- Blotting paper, cotton wool, foam, lint, muslin.
- Cress, mustard, alfalfa, pea seeds.
- Runner beans, French beans, mung beans.
- Tops of carrot, parsnip, turnip, beetroot, pineapple, onion.
- Acorns, conkers.
- Flowers in a vase.
- A wilting plant.

Sharing

- What does it feel like to walk in the rain? What do you have to wear to go out in the rain? How many of you have been to the seaside? What did you enjoy doing in the water? Have you been on a boat?
- What lives in the water? How many names of sea-fish do you know?
- What lives in ponds?
- What does water sound like at the seaside? What does it sound like when it comes out of a tap?
- (*Showing the wilting plant*) What has happened to this plant? What does it need?

Play

Look at and play with the things in the setting.

Bible story
MARK 4. 35–41

'Isn't it a wonderful evening?' said Peter. He was with his friends, by the lake. They were fishermen and they kept their boats on a big lake called the Sea of Galilee. It had been a very busy day and Jesus had been talking to lots of people. Peter, James, John and Andrew suggested it would be a change for them all to go out on a boat across the lake to a quiet spot where they could rest.

They were out in the middle of the lake, rowing steadily along; the boat was rocking gently and Jesus was soon asleep. Sometimes round this lake the weather changed very quickly and a sudden storm could blow up. One minute the water would be smooth and calm and the next the waves would get bigger and bigger as the wind blew harder and harder and boats were tossed about, no matter how hard people rowed.

It happened on this evening, and soon the men were getting rather frightened and they didn't seem able to row so well, as the boat went up and down on the huge waves. While everyone else was shouting and telling each other what they ought to do, Jesus stayed fast asleep. Then he woke up and saw what was going on. The boat was filling up with water.

'Let's be quiet. The wind will drop and the water will be calm,' he said. 'If you all row together, it will be much better. These storms stop as quickly as they start. Look, the waves are not so big and the water is getting calmer already.' He was right. Soon they were on their way again across the lake.

Peter turned to Jesus and said, 'You are amazing. You've never been a fisherman and you're not used to the lake, but you know just what to do. You're very special.'

Activities

- Guess sounds from a home-produced tape of water noises (e.g. flushing toilet, running tap, boiling kettle, dripping tap, washing hands, filling the bath, filling a milk bottle, and outside noises if possible) [P].
- Fill a plastic garden trough with water. Make a simple bridge from card and fasten it across the trough. Play 'Pooh sticks', blowing the sticks or using a hair dryer to create moving water.
- Magnetic fishing.

Planting

- Place vegetable and pineapple tops in shallow containers of water. Keep in a warm, light position.
- Wrap conkers and acorns in wet cotton wool and keep in a plastic bag. Watch the shoots grow. Then put them in a pot to watch the trees grow.
- Help the children to plant beans and peas in jam jars lined with blotting paper.
- Grow some cress.
- Cut about 30 cm from a pair of tights. Tie one end. Fill with sawdust (available from pet shops) and grass seed. Tie the other end. Put on a dish. Keep moist. Watch it grow.

Music and rhymes

SONGS

'One day when we were fishing' (*BBP*)

'Five little speckled frogs' (*Apusskidu*)

RHYMES

Here is the sea, the wavy sea.
Here is the boat, and here is me.
All the little fishes down below
Wriggle their tails and away they go.

This Little Puffin

(*Use actions*)

Two little boats are on the sea.
All is calm as calm can be.
Gently the wind begins to blow.
Two little boats rock to and fro.
Loudly the wind begins to shout.
Two little boats are tossed about.
Gone is the wind, the storm, the rain.
Two little boats sail on again.

This Little Puffin

Drama and movement

- Sing and act to the song 'Row, row, row your boat'.
- Play the tune of 'Sailing' or other 'watery' music and pretend to be different kinds of boats (e.g. yachts, motor boats, hydrofoils, slow barges, canal boats, canoes).

Another story

It was Sunday morning and Alice and her mother were getting ready to go to church. When they were about to leave the house, Mum went into the kitchen and picked up a bucket.

'What are you doing with that bucket, Mummy?'

'I'll tell you in a minute. Can you find the one you were playing with yesterday?'

As they were going to church Mum explained, 'Mr Brown rang up last night, and he would like us to help him in the service today. It's a special service and he s going to talk about water.'

Alice still thought it was funny to be taking buckets to church, and she wondered what they were going to do with them. When they got near the church they met Alice's friend Sue and her mother carrying buckets, and then along came Katy and her family with buckets too. It was getting more and more mysterious.

Mr Brown explained to everyone that in some places there were houses without taps, and so water had to be fetched from a well or even a river. This was usually a job for the women and girls, who started helping when they were quite small. He asked the mothers who'd brought buckets to come out to the front and to bring their daughters with them.

'We'll all pretend we live in a village in Africa. You are going to fetch water for us. The well is a long way away, about half an hour's walk. The best way to carry buckets of water is on your heads. Can you do that?'

The water carriers looked at each other, quite worried.

Mr Brown said, 'To help you with the carrying, I've made you each a little mat out of a scarf. You put the mat on your head and balance the bucket on top.'

'Can we hold the bucket with our hands?' asked Alice.

'Oh yes,' laughed Mr Brown, 'because water is so precious here in this village, we don't want to lose a drop.'

Then he sent them off on their half-hour walk to the well. Actually he said they needn't take that long. The people in church would sing two hymns and pretend they were waiting an hour for the water to arrive.

The women and girls walked out of the church and went to the well. There wasn't a real one,

of course, so they filled their buckets in the kitchen – at least they put some water in each bucket, as much as they could lift easily to balance on their heads. They set off back into church and found they had to walk very slowly and carefully so as not to spill any water.

Mr Brown asked them how they had managed. Sue's mother said, 'We only walked for a few minutes carrying the buckets and found it very difficult, so I don't know how the women and girls in Africa manage doing it every day.'

'It makes me thankful that I can just turn a tap on,' said Alice's mother. 'I think I shall be more careful not to waste it now, it's so precious.'

Then everyone in church joined in prayers to say thank you to God for water and to remember the people who have such difficulty in getting the water they need every day of their lives.

Story books

- Shirley Hughes, *Mr McNally's Hat*, Walker, 1983.
- Shirley Hughes, *Out and About*, Walker, 1988.
- *Water*, Moonlight Publishing/First Discovery, 1991.
- Brian Wildsmith, *Fishes*, Oxford University Press, 1985.

Prayers

Float candles or nightlights on a bowl of water. Sit on the floor round the bowl. Hold hands and say thank-you prayers for water, remembering those who have to carry their water a long way.

Preparation

Make the audio tape of water sounds and prepare the artificial rain.

Note

Water is looked at from two different aspects, which could be used consecutively.

Water is useful

Aim

To help children to think about the many uses of water and to be grateful for it.

Setting

- Place Christian Aid and Water Aid pictures around the room.

REFRESHING AREA

- Ice cubes (e.g. plain, coloured with food dye, frozen with fruit or mint etc.).
- A jug of water, straws, plastic glasses, a small bottle of squash.
- Iced tea in a tea pot, with cups, mugs etc.

CLEANSING AREA

- A washing-up bowl, soap, a towel, sponges, flannels, dish-mops, washing-up liquid, washing powder, warm water.
- Things which need washing – cups, saucers, clothes.
- Toothbrushes [P], toothpaste and a glass.

DISCOVERING AREA

- A bowl of water with a selection of small familiar items for experimenting with floating and sinking (e.g. a stone, a cork), jars of water, food colouring, droppers.
- Clear plastic cups of water, a bucket, small containers of coffee, sugar, Oxo, rice, salt, sand, epsom salts, snow (if winter), freezer-frost.
- Funnels, sieves, a water wheel, small plastic bottles, plastic jugs, a bowl of soapy water with straws, a doll's tea set, plastic trays.

GROWING AREA

- As last time, but growing!

Sharing

What do we use water for? What is water like? (*Pour water from a jug and watch how the water comes out – not straight, but in a spiral.*) What happens to water when it gets very cold or very hot? (*Show ice cubes and flask of boiling water.*) What happens to water when you have finished with it? Where did people get their water from before they had taps?

Play

Use all the things in the setting to discover something about the properties of water.

Bible story
JUDGES 7. 2–7

'Gideon, Gideon, what are we going to do? We are very frightened!'

The people of Israel knew their enemy was coming to fight them and that there would be a big battle. Gideon was the captain of their army and they all trusted him. He was always ready to do his job. He wore a shield and carried a sword so that no one could take him by surprise. But Gideon had a problem. He didn't have enough soldiers to help him.

'Don't worry,' he said. 'I will send messengers to ask as many men as possible to meet me by the river.'

Hundreds and hundreds and hundreds of men turned up and Gideon looked at them all. He only wanted 300. He'd got far too many! How could he choose the best ones? Then he remembered something his father had told him when he was young. His father said, 'When you grow up to be a soldier, remember that you cannot fight well when you are thirsty, but often the only water you will find will be a stream. Then, there's a special rule you must remember. Never put your sword and shield down and kneel to drink. Your enemy might creep up from behind and get you! Always keep your sword in one hand, scoop some water in the other hand, and drink it standing up. That way you can be looking out for the enemy.'

God told Gideon to use this as a test to help him choose his soldiers. He called to the men, 'It's a hot day. It's going to be thirsty work. Go and get a drink from the river before we set off.'

The men rushed to the river. Gideon watched carefully. Sure enough, some of the men knelt down to drink, but other men scooped the water into their hands and stood to drink. 'These are the men I need,' said Gideon. 'They will always be ready and on the look-out all the time.' He was right, and they did win the battle.

Activities

- Children make drinks, pouring their own water and squash (blackcurrant or other flavour).
- Wash hands and clean teeth.
- Fill empty milk bottles with different amounts of water to make sounds and 'music'.
- Make jelly, replacing most of the water with ice-cubes for quick setting.

Music and rhymes

SONGS

'Water of life' (chorus only) (*Come and Praise*)

'I love the pit, pit, patter of the raindrops' (*BBP*)

RHYMES

'Jack and Jill'

'Rub a dub dub'

Bubble, said the kettle,
Bubble, said the pot,
Bubble, bubble, bubble, bubble,
We are very, very hot.

Shall I take you off the fire?
No, you need not trouble.
That is just the way we talk
Bubble, bubble, bubble, bubble.

I'm a little tea pot, short and stout,
Here's my handle, here's my spout.
When I get the steam up, hear me shout,
Tip me up and pour me out.

Traditional

Mother's washing, mother's washing,
Rub, rub, rub.
Picked up Johnny's little shirt
And threw it in the tub.

Daddy's washing, daddy's washing
Scrub, scrub, scrub.
Picked up Emma's dirty jeans
And threw them in the tub.

It's all finished, it's all finished,
Hip, hip, hooray.
Now we'll have our clothes all clean
To wear another day.

Adapted from This Little Puffin

(*Include as many items of children's clothing as possible in this rhyme.*)

Drama and movement

Act out ways of using water as you sing 'This is the way we pour the drinks/ do the washing/ wash our hands/ clean our teeth/ wash the dishes/ turn on the tap/ have a shower/ have a bath/ wash our hair' etc.

Another story

'There's exciting news in this letter!' said Mum as she read her post. 'A lady from India is coming to stay with us next week. She's called Mrs Sita Jaffrey. That's a different kind of name, isn't it?'

'Will she want to eat chapattis and poppadums?' asked Michael. That surprised the family until he told them he'd been learning about India at school.

'We'll have to find out what Mrs Jaffrey likes to eat when she comes,' said Mum. 'And I think she can sleep in the bedroom with the washbasin in it – that'll be easy for her when we all use the bathroom.'

Mum got the room ready and Michael brought a book from school about India. 'I'll show you how people in India say "hello" to each other,' he said. 'They put their hands together like saying a prayer and do a little bow.'

He and Rachel practised that. Rachel liked looking at the pictures in the book – the lovely brightly coloured saris that the ladies wore, and the funny taxis that were like bicycles with a big basket seat on the back.

'Will Mrs Sita Jaffrey come in one of those?' she asked Mum.

'No, she's coming on the train. We'll go to the station to meet her.'

At the station, they stood on the platform to watch the train come in. Lots of people got off the train and walked past them. Then Rachel spotted someone in a beautiful green sari. 'I think she's here,' she said.

Mum went up to this lady and asked, 'Are you Mrs Sita Jaffrey?'

'Yes, I am. Thank you for coming to meet me,' said the Indian lady. She put down her bag and greeted them with her hands together and with a little bow, just like Michael and Rachel had been practising. They smiled and greeted her in the same way and then between them they carried her bag to the car.

At home Mum showed Mrs Jaffrey to the bedroom and Rachel explained, 'We wanted you to have the room with the washbasin so we wouldn't get in your way in the morning.'

'That's very kind,' said Mrs Jaffrey. 'But you know, I am used to having a jug of water and a bowl at home in India. Because we are always short of water there we don't let water run down the plug-hole when we have finished washing. We take that water to pour on the plants in the garden.'

Mum said, 'It's easy for us to forget that you have to use every drop of water in places where it's very hot and where it doesn't rain very often.'

Michael could hardly wait to ask, 'Do you want to eat chapattis and poppadums while you stay with us?'

Mrs Jaffrey laughed. 'I do like them very much,' she said, 'but I also like the food you eat, and I particularly like your porridge!'

Story books

- Gene Zion, *Harry the Dirty Dog*, Bodley Head, 1960.
- Sarah Garland, *Doing the Washing*, Picture Puffin, 1985.
- Shirley Hughes, *An Evening at Alfie's*, Bodley Head, 1984.

Prayers

- Float candles on a bowl of water as for the previous chapter, and add to them flower heads. Place a pitcher of water beside the bowl.
- Thank God that we have water for drinking and washing, coming to us fresh and clean from taps whenever we want it. Pray for those who have very little water, who do not have fresh, clean water.

Preparation

Each child should bring an apron and a marked toothbrush.

Note

This topic on water concentrates largely on the uses of water and can be linked with the previous one.

Weather

To help children to understand that all the different kinds of weather are part of God's creation.

Setting

- Play weather tapes.
- Create weather displays in different areas of the room.

SUNNY

- A sun on the wall.
- Deckchair, sun-hats, sun glasses, swimsuits, summer clothing.

SNOWY

- Blue paper on the wall, with dabs of white paint to represent snow.
- Snowflakes on windows.
- Gloves, hats, scarves, ear muffs, anoraks, boots, mittens.

RAINY

- A rainbow, black clouds and lightning on the wall.
- Paper clouds as mobiles.
- Raindrops (see Appendix).
- Welly boots, raincoats, rainhats.

Sharing

- What was the weather like when you came today? Did you wear anything special because of the weather? What do you enjoy most when it is wet?
- What do we sometimes see in the sky when it is raining? What colours are in the rainbow? What time of the year

do we have snow? What do you enjoy about the snow?

Play

Dress up, using the setting and everything in it.

Bible story
GENESIS 6. 9 – 8. 19

'Is that a cloud coming over the hills?' thought Noah. Surely it must rain soon; every day was so hot and sunny. The fields around were so dry that the plants were not growing at all. In fact, the seeds he'd planted for next year's harvest hadn't even begun to show above the ground. Noah wasn't sure that the cloud was coming, but he was sure that an idea was getting stronger in his mind. He knew it was God telling him to get ready for something – he was to build an Ark!

An ark was like a large boat, but it seemed ridiculous when there was no water to be seen. What would other people say when he told them what he was going to do? 'I'm sure they'll laugh when they find out it's a boat I'm building,' Noah said to himself, 'but I'm also sure God has a good reason for wanting me to do this.'

He and his family got on with the building of the ark and collecting everything to go in it for themselves, and for all the animals, two of every kind, which were going too. They were all ready. Then it started to rain and rain and rain, all day and all night, on and on and on. Soon there were puddles on the fields which got bigger and bigger; they joined up and became lakes. The ark floated like a boat and everybody got on board. Noah and his family were busy looking after everything – all the children and all the animals *and* trying to keep dry.

The rain went on for days and days and days. 'Will the rain ever stop?' they said to each other. Every day Noah looked at the sky to see if the dark clouds were going away at all. One day he got excited when there seemed to be much less rain, and then suddenly he shouted, 'Come and look, everyone!' There was a most beautiful rainbow across the sky, and the sun was shining again. 'Thank goodness,' they all said. 'Let's thank God,' said Noah. 'We are all safe on the ark; God has looked after us.'

Activities

- Welly walking (see Appendix).
- Collages in appropriate colours for different weather. (Black, grey and white for the winter-type weather, with cotton wool and polystyrene packing slugs. Blue and grey and silver for rainy days; foil for reflections, rainbow colours. Blue, orange, yellow and white for sunny days.)
- Paintings in similar colours.
- A snowball fight (make snowballs by glueing six white cotton-wool balls together with Copydex) [P].
- Beach-ball games and quoits.
- Go out to a local park or open space, dressing up appropriately for the weather. Experience the conditions: watch which way the wind is blowing; fly a kite; see the clouds going across the sky; if it's sunny look at shadows; chase cloud shadows; jump in the puddles!

Music and rhymes

SONGS

'Morning, evening, frost and dew' (*BBP*)

'I like the sunshine' (*BBP*)

'I hear thunder' (*Traditional*)

'Jingle bells'

'The north wind doth blow'

'I can sing a rainbow' (*Apusskidu*)

RHYMES

Marching in our wellingtons
Tramp, tramp, tramp.
Marching in our wellingtons
We won't get damp.
Splashing through the puddles
In the rain, rain, rain.
Splashing through the puddles
Splashing home again.

HPPA

I said 'This way', the wind said 'That' –
'Ho,' said the wind, 'I'll have your hat.'
He took my hat with a shout of glee
And hung it high on the top of a tree.

HPPA

Drama and movement

- Pretend you are splashing, skating, jumping in puddles, sunbathing, swimming, paddling, jumping over the waves, going for a walk on a windy day etc.
- Act out building a snowman by rolling a ball of snow round and round, etc.
- 'One day when we were fishing' (*BBP*). Sing the song and do the actions.

Another story

'Can I go out to play when the rain stops?' Sam asked. His big brother and sister had gone back to school after the summer holidays, and playgroup didn't start again until next week. Sam had played with them most days, so today the house seemed empty and quiet. And it was raining – not a bit, but a lot! Sam watched the raindrops chasing down the windows and saw the puddles on the path getting bigger and bigger.

'I'd like to go out and walk through all the puddles.'

'We'll have to find your wellies, then,' said Dad. 'We've not needed them during the summer.'

They looked all over the place and found them at last, and Sam tried to put them on. He pulled and pulled and pulled, but it was no good – they didn't fit any more.

'Oh well, off to the shops as soon as the rain stops,' said Dad. At last it did stop raining, and they set off.

Sam had to be very careful not to walk through the puddles in his shoes and socks, and they only got a bit wet. At the shop there were so many wellies to choose from: red pairs, blue pairs, even some striped ones. Sam liked the shiny black ones best, and there was a pair that fitted beautifully. The shopkeeper was going to put them in a bag, but Sam said, 'I'd really like to wear them to go home. Can I?' They put his old shoes in the bag and Sam went home in his shiny, black wellies.

Do you think he walked round all the puddles on the way home, or right through the middle of each one?

Story books

- Nick Butterworth and Mick Inkpen, *The Mouse's Tale: Jesus and the Storm*, Marshall Pickering, 1988.
- Stacie Strong, *The Big Book of Noah's Ark*, Candle Books, 1991.
- Sophie Kniffke, *Weather*, Moonlight Publishing, 1990.
- Jan Pienkowski, *Weather*, Puffin, 1983.
- Jan Godfrey, *Why is it Raining?* Tamarind, 1993.
- Reeve Lindeberg, *What is the Sun?* Walker Books, 1995.
- Eugenie Fernandes, *My Sunny Day Book*, Ladybird, 1988.
- Pat Hutchins, *The Wind Blew*, Red Fox, 1994.

 ## Prayers

Have a prayer walk to the different parts of the room.

In the 'sunny' area give thanks for sunshine and remember countries where it gets very hot and very dry.

In the 'rainy' area thank God for rain. Remember people who suffer from floods.

In the 'snowy' area thank God for the fun we have in snow. Remember people who find snowy weather difficult (e.g. old people afraid of falling, car drivers afraid of skidding). Give thanks for the people who clear the roads and make them safe.

Sounds

Setting

Use two areas of the room to represent big sounds and little sounds.

BIG SOUNDS

A drum, a radio, a football rattle, an airhorn, a blowing instrument, an alarm clock, a whistle, a large saucepan with a metal spoon, a microphone amplifier with a speaker, a bicycle bell.

LITTLE SOUNDS

A teaspoon in a cup, little bells, musical box, a milk bottle keyboard, paper to rustle, a ticking clock, a gentle rattle, a shaker with rice in it, milk-bottle tops on a string, a tape of bird songs (playing in the background).

OTHER SOUNDS

A 'walkman' with headphones and a nursery rhyme tape, a children's tape recorder.

Sharing

- Can you think of some little sounds? Can you think of some big sounds? Which sounds do you like best? Which sounds don't you like? Are there any sounds you find a little frightening?
- Listen and see what sounds we can hear. What part of our body helps us to hear the sounds? If our ears do not work properly, what happens? (Put fingers in ears and listen to small sounds.)

- What can people have to help them when they can't hear properly? (If possible invite someone who has a hearing aid to show it to the children.)

Play

Explore the setting and everything in it. Ear plugs may be necessary for some!

Bible story
1 KINGS 19. 12

'Why don't people listen to me?' thought Elijah.

People called Elijah a prophet, because he was able to tell them what God wanted them to do and how they should behave. Sometimes people listened to him, but more often they didn't. Elijah didn't know what to do and he was very sad. 'I don't think I'm any good as a prophet. They won't listen to the messages that God has given me for them. What can I do?'

Elijah decided to go off for a long walk up a high mountain, so that he could think what to do next. This mountain was a very special place for the people of Israel. Perhaps he'd find out there what God was going to do.

He had found a cave and decided to shelter from the hot sun. He had only just settled down when there was the sound of a strong rushing wind which got louder and louder, so that even some stones were moved about by the wind.

'Ah!' thought Elijah, 'perhaps God is going to use the wind to blow down the people who won't behave well.' But the wind stopped as suddenly as it started.

Then the ground began to shake and there was a rumbling noise all around, and Elijah thought, 'This earthquake might be God's way of showing the people how angry he is.' But soon it was still and quiet again.

Next came a crackling sound and a smell of smoke, and there was a big fire all across the

mountain-side. It got quite hot in the cave, but Elijah was quite safe. 'I wonder if fire is going to be the way the people find out how they have made God sad and angry.' Gradually, though, the fire died down and went out.

Elijah sat down at the front of the cave and listened. He couldn't hear anything – not a sound. It was completely quiet and still. Surely nothing would happen now.

Then suddenly he knew what God wanted him to do. He seemed to hear God's voice speaking to him quietly and telling him to go back to the people and to talk to as many of them as he could. God said he would find a new friend to help him as well. Elijah was not so sad now that he knew what he had to do next, but he was a bit surprised that he had heard God in the quiet sound and not in the great big noisy ones.

Activities

- Play 'Chinese whispers'.
- Listen to the pre-prepared tape [P]. Guess what the sounds are and imitate them.
- Provide a variety of plastic or metal containers with lids and a variety of materials for the children to experiment with (e.g. rice, small stones, wood shavings, pasta, nuts, leaves, sand, buttons).
- Use a modern version of Psalm 150 to be read and accompanied by instruments (see *Listen*, Collins).

Music and rhymes

SONGS

'We all march to the beating drum' (*BBP*)

'Hallelu, hallelu, hallelu, hallelujah' (*Junior Praise*)

'Praise the Lord with the sound of a drum' (*Children's Praise*)

'I hear thunder'

RHYMES

What does the clock in the hall say?
Tick-tock, tick-tock.
What does the clock on the wall say?
Tick tock, tick tock, tick tock.
What does my tiny little watch say?
Ticker, ticker, ticker, ticker, ticker.

This Little Puffin

BOOM bang clunk **clang**
Rattle ROAR ring
Clatter CRASH squeak splash
Patter pop ping

Drama and movement

- Act out:
  My wellington boots go splish, splosh, splish, splosh,
  My walking shoes go tip, tap, tip, tap,
  My bedroom slippers make no sound at all.
- Make sounds with your body: clicking fingers, slapping sides, clapping hands, chattering teeth, clicking your tongue, stamping your feet, finger popping in the mouth.

Another story

'It's no good, I can't get to sleep! It's hot and I can see the light through the curtain.' Mum had pinned a piece of dark material over the window to make the bedroom less bright, but tonight it didn't help at all.

Roger could hear lots of different sounds, and they seemed to be keeping him awake. There was the washing-machine droning, Dad's drill rumbling away downstairs, and next door someone was practising the piano. In a garden nearby there seemed to be a barbecue going on, with people singing and talking. None of these sounds were very loud, but Roger wished they would all be quiet.

When Mum came to see if he was still awake, he said to her, 'Tonight, I almost wish I couldn't hear at all.'

Mum said, 'I know what you mean, but I don't really think you'd like that all the time. People who can't hear properly find lots of things very difficult.' She brought Roger a cool drink and sang him some very quiet going-to-sleep songs, and he was soon asleep.

Next day Roger asked Mum how people who can't hear manage, and she said an old friend of hers had come to live nearby, who was like that. She had planned to go and see her, so Roger could come too. 'You'll like my friend Betty,' she said. 'She's great fun, and I don't think she'll mind you asking her about her deafness.'

They went round to have tea with Betty, and Roger was a bit surprised that she seemed the same as everyone else. He and Mum didn't have to talk very loud, but Betty asked them to sit where she could see their faces, because she could lip-read, and they all chatted together quite easily.

Roger noticed that Betty's hands and fingers moved about much more than his and Mum's, so he asked her if she could hand-read as well as lip-read. Betty laughed and told him that lots of people who can't hear

very well learn signs that they do with their hands and fingers. She showed him some easy ones that he could understand and do himself, like fanning yourself for showing you are hot and pretending to yawn to show you are tired.

'I know,' said Betty. 'I'll do some rhymes with my hands and see if you can guess them.' Roger guessed 'Incy-wincy spider' and 'Hickory, Dickory Dock' very quickly but it took longer to work out 'Two little dicky-birds sat upon a wall'.

On the way home, Roger said he had had a lovely time and he liked Betty very much. 'But I'm glad I *can* hear sounds,' he said, ' even if I don't always like them and they sometimes keep me awake.'

Shall we work out signs for some of the rhymes and songs you know? Then you'll know how lucky we are that we can hear.

Story books

- Rachel Isadora, *I Hear*, Picture Lions, 1987.
- Philip Hawthorne and Jenny Tyler, *Who's Making That Noise?*, Usborne, 1994.

Prayers

Play some quiet music in the background. Move to the 'big sounds area'. Say prayers of thanks for being able to hear big sounds (like ...). Shout 'Hallelujah!' Move to the 'little sounds area'. Say prayers of thanks for being able to hear little sounds (like ...). Whisper 'Hallelujah!' Move to the middle and say prayers for those who cannot hear.

Preparation

Record on a tape some domestic and community sounds.

Colours

Aim

To raise children's awareness of the huge variety of colours which are all around them

Setting

In each corner of the room have small collections of objects of different colours. Use drapes and natural materials as well as manufactured objects. Try to have a variety of textures. Everything must be safe for children to handle.

RED CORNER

A red drape, toys, kitchen objects, shoes, boots, clothes, containers, poinsettias, etc.

GREEN CORNER

A green drape, toys, green vegetables, plants, ferns, moss etc.

YELLOW CORNER

A yellow drape, toys, yellow fruit and vegetables, gourds, yellow flowers etc.

BLUE CORNER

A blue drape, a hat, a scarf, household utensils, flowers, toys etc.

MULTI-COLOURED AREA

In the centre of the room put a multi-coloured table, a drape, toys, clothes etc. containing a vivid mixture of colours (e.g. hundreds and thousands, jelly babies, rainbow items etc.). Have a range of kaleidoscopes. In the centre have a pile of small red, green, yellow and blue items (e.g. bricks).

Sharing

What colours are you wearing today? If you're wearing green, stand up. If you're wearing red, clap your hands etc. What's your favourite colour? What can you think of that is red, yellow etc. which is not in the room? (E.g. the sun, fire, grass, the sky.)

Play

Investigate the items in the corners. Collect objects of the appropriate colours from the centre and add them to the corners.

Bible story

GENESIS 37. 3

Rachel was really clever at sewing. It was a good thing, because there was a very big family to look after. There were twelve boys, so you can imagine how busy she was with all of them. There were no shops at that time, where you could go and buy new clothes, so Rachel used to go to the market to buy pieces of material. Then she'd cut out and sew shirts and coats out of those pieces.

The older ones among the brothers were quite tall, so Rachel had to buy big pieces of material to make their coats. Then there were others not so tall, so the pieces of material for their coats were not so big. The two youngest of the brothers were Joseph and little Benjamin.

Rachel had just finished making a coat for each of the brothers, all different sizes and in different colours – that is, except for Joseph's and Benjamin's coats. She had a small piece of material left that was just big enough to make a little coat for Benjamin.

'But I don't know where I'm going to find a piece of material to make into a coat for you, Joseph,' she said. 'All I've got now are the pieces that are left over from making coats for your brothers.'

Joseph's father, Jacob, looked at the pieces laid out on the table – brown ones, green ones and grey ones, some striped pieces and some with a mixture of colours. 'Could you make Joseph a coat out of these pieces if they were joined together?' he asked. 'It would be a coat of lots of different colours.'

Rachel took quite a long time to make this coat, because there was so much sewing to do, but she finished it at last. It had a brown back, one big green sleeve and one big grey one, and the front of the coat was a real mixture of colours, with a striped pocket.

Joseph was so pleased, and he walked about in his new coat very proudly. 'It's the best coat in the family!' he said to his brothers.

Jacob and Rachel told him to stop showing off. 'Just because you are wearing a coat that is different, it doesn't make you any more important than anyone else around here.'

Activities

- Make bead necklaces of different colours.
- Sort bricks, beads etc. into small containers.
- Mix paint, using fingers to blend the colours into other colours.
- Make patterns with sticky paper squares. Use gummed shapes to make pictures.
- Collect cellophane sweet wrappers and use them to make a picture [P].
- Look through a kaleidoscope.

Music and rhymes

SONGS

'Who put the colours in the rainbow?' (*Come and Praise*)

'Sing a rainbow' (*Apusskidu*)

'Who put the white in the clouds so free?' (*BBP*)

'The green dress' (*The Music Box Songbook*)

'The wedding dress song' (*The Music Box Songbook*)

RHYMES

Roses are red
Violets are blue
Sugar is sweet
And so are you.

Traditional

Grapes are purple, and grapes are green,
Tomatoes are shiny red.
Lemons are yellow, plums are blue,
But oranges – are orange.

Corn is yellow, beetroot is red,
Potatoes are nobbly and brown.
Carrots are orange, turnips are white,
And greens – are green.

Drama and movement

Ask the children to think of a colour and the movements they might make to go with it. Here are some suggestions:

- Red: being like flames, being hot, being angry.
- Blue: in a boat on a calm sea, on a rough sea.
- Green: lying on the grass on a summer afternoon. (What does it feel like? What can you see? What can you hear?)

- Yellow: being like the sun spreading its rays, being happy, being friendly.

Another story

'Are you awake yet, Jessica?' asked Amy. 'Isn't it exciting?! It's Aunty Pam's wedding day!' Jessica's pretty blue bridesmaid's dress was hanging on the cupboard door.

'What colour dress did you have when you were a bridesmaid?' Jessica asked Amy.

'It was pink, and I had pink flowers in my hair, and a little posy of pink flowers to carry,' Amy told her. 'You are lucky, Jessica, to be a bridesmaid today. It's good fun going in the big cars, everyone taking photographs and saying how nice you look. I did get a bit fed up with all the standing around, but I still wish I was going to be a bridesmaid again.'

Just then Mum came into the bedroom and she saw Amy's face looking a bit sad. 'Come on,' she said. 'It's going to be a lovely day for us all, and we want it to be specially happy for Aunty Pam and Uncle Bill.'

Soon it was time for everyone to get ready. Jessica went to Aunty Pam's house to get dressed in her blue bridesmaid's dress with the other bridesmaids. Dad and Mum put on their wedding clothes. Dad put on his best grey suit, his rainbow waistcoat and matching tie, with very shiny black shoes. Mum put on her new sea-green dress and hat.

When Amy looked at herself in the long mirror in her new creamy coloured flowered dress, she was pleased that she looked quite grown up. Then there was a real surprise. Mum had bought a straw hat for Amy, and she had put cream and blue ribbons round it and sewn on a little posy of blue flowers.

The church was full of people in beautiful clothes. Such a lot of different colours! It was a lovely wedding and they all had a really good time. There were lots of photographs of Aunty Pam in her white dress and Uncle Bill in his grey suit and ruby-red waistcoat. Mum said her favourite photograph was one of Jessica and Amy together, laughing at Dad wearing her green hat.

It was Junior Church the next day, and Amy wore her new dress and hat. She wore it the next Sunday and the Sunday after that. I wonder if she went to bed in her hat too!

Story books

- Roy Etherton, *The Day it Rained in Colours*, Lion, 1976.
- P.M. Valat and Sylvane Perols, *Colours*, Moonlight Publishing, 1990.
- Therida Woodford, *My Colorful Day*, Happy Cat Publications, 1993.
- John Burningham, *Colours*, Sainsbury Walker Books, 1985.

(Look in your local library – there will be many books about colour.)

Prayers

Ask each child to choose a strip of crêpe paper in a colour (provide a wide variety to choose from). Sing 'Halle, halle, halle' (*Many and Great*, Wild Goose Worship) or other songs of praise, waving the strips in the air. Join them together by twisting them (the children will need help). Hold them as you say prayers of thanks for blue things, red things etc.

Black and white

Aim

To help the children to have positive attitudes to both black and white.

Setting

Make a zebra crossing from black and white paper. It should be big enough for the children to walk on. Then create three areas within the room:

WHITE AREA

Against a white background (e.g. a white sheet) place some black objects (e.g. wellies, shoes, gloves, bags, ornaments, coal or coke, charcoal, a black furry toy, black playdough, peppercorns, prunes, black and white photographs of black children or adults).

BLACK AREA

Against a black background (e.g. a black bin-bag) place some white objects (e.g. a plate, a cup, a candle, paper, a sock, a shirt, shoes, a towel, a bottle of milk, daisies, lilies, a spring onion, soap, cooking fat, salt, sugar, natural yoghurt, white playdough, black-and-white photographs of white children or adults).

BLACK AND WHITE AREA

Against a background of newsprint place some black and white objects (e.g. a keyboard, books in black and white, dominoes, a die, a clockface, a minister's black shirt and clerical collar, black and white material or garments, ornaments, a football, good black and white photographs, reverse printing (i.e. white on black), Pingu the penguin or a toy panda.

Sharing

What are you wearing that is black or white? What else can you think of that is black or white? What happens if you mix black and white paint together?

Play

Use the setting and everything in it.

Bible story
1 KINGS 17. 4–5

'Stop it!' said Elijah, 'stop being so unkind to each other. Stop calling each other names.' But it didn't make any difference, and the people got angrier and angrier with Elijah. In fact the people got so angry with Elijah that he was afraid that he was not very safe in the town.

Then Elijah thought he heard God telling him to get out into the hilly country by himself. He didn't have time to take any food with him, so he wondered what he would eat, but he was sure God would look after him.

He found a quiet place and sat by a stream. It had clear, bubbling water which he could drink, but he was very hungry and rather lonely. There were some dry trees and dusty bushes on the hillside, but he could not see any birds or animals.

Suddenly, he did see something, far away in the distance. It looked like some small black dots in the sky, above the hills. They got bigger and bigger as they came nearer and nearer. Elijah could see they were very big, black birds – big, black ravens – and they seemed to be carrying something white in their beaks. Elijah was very frightened. They came very close, flapping their wings all around him. Then they landed at his feet. He didn't know what to do, but suddenly he noticed that the white things in their beaks were pieces of bread! Elijah knelt down.

'Thank you, God,' he said. 'I shan't be hungry any more.'

Activities

- Use thick white paint on black paper and thick black paint on white paper. Use large brushes and large sheets of paper.
- Collage – white on black: doilies, lace, fabric, cotton wool, tissues, tissue paper, wool.
- Collage – black on white: net, wool, fabric, scraps of lace, tissue paper.
- Chalking on black paper, using charcoal on white paper.

Music and rhymes

SONGS

'You are loved by God' (*BBP*)

'The ink is black, the page is white' (first verse only) (*Come and Praise*)

RHYMES

Big black spider,
Climbing up the wall
Never, never, never,
Seems to fall.
Yet I always fall
When I climb the garden gate,
I've only got two legs
And he's got eight.

HPPA

It's so cold this morning
Perhaps there'll soon be snow.
Put on your boots and warm clothes
And outside we will go.
Now the snow is falling
Everywhere looks white
Roll yourself a snowball
And have a snowball fight.

HPPA

The Snowman

He shines like a candle
and melts slowly

He is white and black
and gets smaller all the time

He is as white as feathers
and white horses and snow

He glows in the dark
like a glow-worm

He stands on a flat place
and makes a shadow in the light

He crumples in a circle
like a circus tent

He turns to ice and slush
like a camel's hump

He runs away like milk
and melts like moonlight in sunshine

In the morning he has gone
like the moon.

Children's poetry workshop,
in Another Very First Poetry Book

Drama

- Mime all kinds of activities related to the black and white objects (e.g. build a snowman, kick a football, hit a golf ball, throw a dice, hit a table-tennis ball).
- Pretend to be different black, white or black and white animals. Ask the children to think of an animal and to act it out for the others to guess.

Another story

'What's your favourite colour? I like . . . What's yours?'

Suzy, who was nearly five, liked black best of all. She always chose black when she could – black shiny shoes, black liquorice sweets and black felt pens. Their cat, Midnight, was black too.

For birthday and Christmas presents she'd already had a blackboard and a lovely black baby doll with curly black hair.

Suzy and Mum were making marzipan animals to go on her birthday cake. There was a small piece of marzipan left, so Mum gave it to Suzy and asked her what colour she'd like it to be. Guess what Suzy said. You're right – black! So they mixed drops of different food colours together and got a beautiful black. Suzy rolled and pinched the marzipan into different shapes. 'I'm going to make a little black rat,' she said. 'It will look super on the white icing – because what I want more than anything for my birthday is a real, black rat.'

Mum sighed. 'I've explained to you that we can't have a rat in the house with Midnight here, because cats and rats don't like each other. Try and think of something else, Suzy.'

But Suzy couldn't. She'd always wanted a black rat to play with. That evening, Mum was telling Aunty Nora about this and how she didn't know what to get for Suzy's present. 'Leave it to me,' said Aunty Nora. 'I've just had an idea.'

Suzy was very excited the night before her birthday, and she was rather surprised when Mum put a white pillowcase on the end of the bed. 'It's ready for your present,' she said. 'We can do this for birthdays as well as for Christmas, you know. Now off you go to sleep.'

Suzy found this very difficult. She kept on wondering what would be in the pillowcase in the morning – something black, she hoped, peeping out. At last she dropped off to sleep.

In the morning she remembered it was her birthday as soon as she woke up, and she remembered the pillowcase. What was that black pointed thing, like a long nose, poking out of the top of the white pillowcase? It felt soft when Suzy put her hand into the pillowcase. What do you think she pulled out? It

was a toy black rat with a velvety coat, bright beady eyes, silky whiskers and a long tail!

Suzy cuddled and stroked her rat and talked to it. 'I'll call you Sooty,' she said. 'And you can come to my birthday party and meet the little black rat on my cake, among the candles. It's black on white, like you were on my bed.'

Clever Aunty Nora had made the rat out of her old black velvet skirt. Wasn't that a good idea?

Story books

- Marjorie Flack, The *Angus* books, Picture Puffin, 1973 –.
- Eric Hill, The *Spot* books, Heinemann, 1982 –.

Prayers

- Stand on the black stripes on the zebra crossing. Pray for black people – those we know and those we don't.
- Stand on the white stripes. Pray for white people – those we know and those we don't.
- Put one foot on a white stripe and one on a black stripe. Thank God for making us different. Thank God for loving us all the same.

Circles

Aim

Through the exploration of circles to help children to begin to understand something of God's concern for groups and for individuals.

81

Setting

Put chairs in a circle. Decorate the walls with coloured circles of different sizes and textures. Spread hoops around the room, containing some of the following:

- Plates, saucers, trays and mats.
- Bangles, necklaces, rings and hooped ear-rings.
- Biscuits, cucumber rings (cut thin so that they look like circles rather than cylinders), tomato rings, slices of orange, flat mushrooms, biscuits, slices of Swiss roll, slices of salami, onion slices, Polos, refreshers.
- Indian bells, tambourines, cymbals.
- A frisby, tiddlywinks, spinners, draughts.
- Flat lids and bottle tops.
- Coins, buttons and badges.
- Compact discs.

Sharing

- What circles can you find . . . in the room? on your body? on your clothes?
- Which are the smallest? Which are the biggest?
- What circles did you see on your way here?
- Which circles move? Which circles have no middles?

Play

Use the setting and everything in it for sorting, matching and talking.

Bible story

LUKE 15. 8–10: THE LOST COIN

'Oh no!' said Dorcas. 'I've lost one! Where can it be?' Dorcas was taking off her beautiful, precious head-dress. It was decorated with round, gold pieces which looked like coins, but one of them was missing. 'What have I been doing today?' she said. 'I've rolled up the bed mats, I've swept the floor, I've made some bread, I've fed the animals, I've been to the well to get water, I've done some washing in the stream and laid it out to dry. Where is my coin? It could be anywhere. Where do I start to look?'

She called to her friend Ruth and told her what had happend. 'Why are you making such a fuss?' said Ruth. 'It's only one that you've lost.'

'But it's precious!' said Dorcas. 'I can't bear to lose even one. I'm going to search until I find it.'

Dorcas began to look. She unrolled the bed mats and shook them. She searched through the flour in the bin. She checked the troughs the animals fed from. She swept the floor. But it was no use – the coin was nowhere to be found.

Her house was dark, with tiny windows, so she lit her little oil lamp. She shone it slowly and carefully all around the room. Suddenly she saw something gleaming in a dark corner. She looked more closely. Her coin was there – it was found!

She rushed round to see Ruth. 'I'm so happy!' she called out. 'I've found my lost coin.'

Every one of Dorcas's coins was important. In the same way, every one of us is important to God.

Activities

- Have a treasure hunt using chocolate gold coins which can be collected and then shared (if you know that these are safe for your group), or 1p or 2p coins.

- Use circular paper of different sizes for painting.
- Play musical circles using circles of paper rather than mats.
- Make a collage with circles of different textures.
- Print with circular objects (e.g. jam-jar tops, etc.).
- Cook circular things (e.g. biscuits).
- Make a circular salad using cucumber, radish, beetroot, carrot, spring onion and hard-boiled egg.
- Play parachute games.

Music and rhymes

SONGS

'The wheels on the bus' (*Okki Tokki Unga*)

'Here we go round the mulberry bush'

'Ring a ring of roses'

'God has put a circle round us' (*BBP*)

'Round and round the circle goes' (*BBP*)

RHYMES

Mix a pancake, stir a pancake,
Pop it in the pan.
Fry a pancake, toss a pancake,
Catch it if you can.

Come Follow Me

Porridge is bubbling,
Bubbling hot,
Stir it round
And round in the pot.
The bubbles plip
The bubbles plop.
It's ready to eat
All bubbling hot.

Sally go round the sun,
Sally go round the moon.
Sally go round the chimney pot
On a Sunday/ Monday/ Tuesday . . . afternoon.

Traditional

Round and round the garden
Like a teddy bear.
One step, two step,
Jump up in the air.

Traditional

Five little men in a flying saucer
Flew round the world one day.
They looked from left to right of it,
Could not stand the sight of it,
So one man flew away.

Four little men etc. . . . .

HPPA

Drama and movement

- Encourage the children to make circles with different parts of the body – whole body, head, arms, fingers, legs, feet, mouth, tongue etc.
- Make circles in twos, fours, sixes and the whole group.
- Skip in a circle. By moving in and out make the circle small or big.
- Do the 'Hokey cokey'.

Another story

'Is there anything else for the washing machine before I shut the door?' called Mum. Everyone in the family was going round looking for things that needed washing. Josie brought the tee-shirts and socks from her room, David found his football shorts that were really muddy under his bed. There were the aprons that hung behind the kitchen door, and someone brought in the old rug that was used for playing outside and for picnics.

Paul was nearly three years old, and he joined in and arrived with a bundle of things off his bed. It was nearly as big as he was! There was no time to sort it all out, so in it all went – into the washing machine with the washing powder and the blue stuff that makes everything soft.

Paul liked to watch when the machine started up and the soapy water got more and more bubbly. Sometimes he could see a bit of blue tee-shirt or a yellow sock going round before it was whisked away again. Today he thought he saw something small, round and black, and he watched very carefully. Now there were two small, round, black things close together with some pale brown fur. 'That's my teddy!' he called out. 'How did he get in there? Please stop the machine and get him out!'

'We can't do that,' explained his Mum. 'We'll have to wait for the whole wash to finish.'

Paul was really worried as he thought of how dizzy he felt if he twirled round and round and round. Teddy seemed to be going even faster. 'Will he be all right?' he asked.

'He'll certainly be very clean,' said Josie.

'And we can find out if his fur is really soft like they say on the TV,' said David.

Paul waited anxiously for the wash to end. When Teddy came out, he was lovely and clean *and* his fur was very soft, but he was too damp to cuddle. 'How can we get him dry, though?' said Paul.

Everyone laughed when Dad said, 'We won't put him in the tumble-drier, anyway.'

'No,' Mum suggested, 'a quiet, warm place by the radiator or in the airing cupboard would be best after all that spinning and whirling around.'

Paul agreed. 'But I wonder how he got in there?'

What do you think?

Story books

- Pierre Marie Valat, *Shapes*, Moonlight Publishing, 1995.
- Nick Butterworth & Mick Inkpen, *Ten Silver Coins*, Marshall Pickering, 1989.
- Daniel Hochstatter, *Sammy Searches for Shapes and Sizes*, Nelson, 1994.
- Debbie Trafton O'Neal, *The Lost Coin*, Judson, 1993.

Prayers

Prepare pictures of people (using a wide range of images) cut into circles. Ask the children to choose one, to place it on a circular worship centre and to gather round in a circle, holding hands. Pray for the people in the pictures and then, in turn, for the people each side of them.

Notes

This theme can be linked to Advent with the preparation and lighting of the Advent ring. In this case, link as many activities as possible to the coming of Christmas (e.g. circular Christmas decorations, paper chains). Consider using the Spheres theme which follows.

Spheres

Aim

To use the concept of spheres to develop in the children a greater sense of awe and wonder in the created world.

Introduction

You may want to use this theme on its own or as a follow-up to the theme of Circles. It can also be adapted to be used in the period immediately before Christmas.

Setting

Gather together a selection of spheres, suspending some if possible:

- A tree branch with polystyrene or pressed-paper spheres and Christmas baubles (at Christmas use a Christmas tree).
- Bunches of balloons and spherical Japanese lanterns.
- A large bowl of oranges, grapefruit, small melons, apples, tomatoes, cherries, brussel sprouts.
- Cat bells, harness bells, maracas, drumsticks and strikers with spherical ends.
- A large inflatable ball, a beach ball, balls of different sizes (hang in a large net or hammock).
- A globe and, if possible, an earth ball.
- Collect washing powder balls (thoroughly washed) and fill them with small, round, edible items (e.g. glacé cherries, cocktail onions, cherry tomatoes, Maltesers, peas).
- Marbles in a jar.
- Mustard seeds, poppy seeds and other seeds (with insect viewers).
- Pictures and posters of the earth taken from space.

Sharing

- Give each child a marble or small ball. Ask them to look at them carefully. What colours are in them? How do they feel? What other things are the same shape? (E.g. frozen peas, sweetcorn, the moon.) Do you know the name of this shape (sphere)?
- Show the globe. Ask the children what it is. Look at how much water there is and how much land. Do the children know where we are on the globe?

Play

Explore all the things in the setting. Make the balls available if appropriate.

Bible story

Genesis 1. 31

'7, 6, 5, 4, 3, 2, 1, lift off! We have lift off!' The spaceship *Apollo 11* was on its way to the moon. There were three astronauts on board – Buzz, Neil and Mike. They were very busy working the controls and talking to the people back on the earth. They were very excited because they hoped to be the first people to land on the moon. They had often seen it at night like a shining white ball, or a sort of banana-shape, in the dark sky. Soon they would be able to see what it was really like.

They were able to look out to see the moon getting larger and larger as they got nearer and nearer. Then Buzz decided to look back the other way, to where they had come from. He gasped with surprise. There was the earth, a round sphere, thousands of miles below them, getting smaller and smaller. It was blue, green and red, like a ball floating in space. It was *so* beautiful.

'Come and look,' he called to Neil and Mike. 'Look at our earth down there, amongst all those twinkling stars.'

'Isn't it amazing to think that that is where all our families live, and millions of other people as well,' said Neil.

Buzz looked again. He remembered the words from the Bible: 'God saw everything that he had made, and indeed, it was very good.' He knew that the first thing he must do when he landed on the moon was to say thank you to God.

 ## Activities

- Paint with marbles. Make a small pool of paint. Roll marbles through it onto paper.
- Decorate oasis balls with greenery, dried flowers, silk flowers, bows and ribbons.
- Make Christingles (see Appendix).
- Make chocolate truffles (see Appendix).
- Invite a juggler to perform for the children.
- Plant mustard seeds.
- Blow bubbles.

 ## Music and rhymes

SONGS

'O what a wonderful world' (*BBP*)

'Big Blue Planet' (*BBP*)

'God who made the earth' (*Junior Praise*, verses 1-3)

I love the sun,
It shines on me.
God made the sun
And God made me.

I love the moon,
It shines on me.
God bless the moon
and God bless me.

Gwen F.Smith, from Someone's Singing, Lord

Bouncing balls go up and down,
Up and down, up and down.
Red and yellow, green and brown,
Bouncing balls go up and down.

HPPA

Five little peas in a pea pod pressed,
One grew, two grew, and so did all the rest.
They grew and they grew, and never stopped
Until at last that pea pod popped.

HPPA

This is the way we kick the ball
Kick the ball, kick the ball.
This is the way we kick the ball
On this happy morning.

Traditional, adapted

(*Ask for suggestions for other verses, e.g. throwing, hitting, catching, bowling.*)

 ## Drama and movement

- Pretend to blow bubbles and to try to catch them as they fly away.
- Pretend to play with a ball in different ways – bowling, kicking, throwing, catching, juggling.

Another story

'That was a good throw,' said Peter. Susan was learning to join in ball games with her brother and sister. She was really looking forward to summer-time, when she could play football, cricket and basketball with them. Susan liked the big soft balls best because they were easy to catch.

One morning Susan fell over and hurt her leg quite badly. She had to go to hospital and have photographs, called X-rays, taken of the bone in her leg. It was broken, so the doctors and their helpers put a huge white plaster on, which was quite heavy on her leg. 'It's bad luck, Susan,' said the doctor. 'You won't be able to run about for a few weeks, I'm afraid.'

Poor Susan! She just had to sit and watch everyone else playing football and cricket. She could still catch and throw balls a bit, but it wasn't nearly as much fun. 'I wish there was a ball game that I could play sitting down,' she said to her Mum. The family all tried to think of something she could do, but no luck.

Then Gran turned up one day with a little tub of special soapy water, and she showed Susan how to blow bubbles. Susan practised and practised, and soon she could blow quite big bubbles, which floated away and shone with rainbow colours in the sunshine.

The only trouble was that it was no good trying to catch them – these bubbles popped as soon as anything touched them. Gran explained that each bubble was a perfect sphere – until it popped!

'I hope my leg will be better soon, so I can play proper ball games again,' Susan said. 'But these bubble balls are certainly the prettiest ones I've ever played with.'

Story books

- Michael Forster, *God's Wonderful World*, Autumn House, 1992.
- Nick Butterworth and Mick Inkpen, *Wonderful Earth*, Hunt & Thorpe, 1990.
- David Lloyd, *The Ball*, Walker, 1991.

- Pierre Lindbergh, *What is the Sun?* Walker, 1994.
  There are wonderful colour photographs (from postcard size upwards) of the earth taken from space, including the cover of *Big Blue Planet*.

 ## Prayers

On a table place strips of red crêpe paper or ribbon across each other to meet in the middle and radiate out like the spokes of a wheel. Fasten them in the centre with a pin or some Blu-tack, and put there a lit Christingle. Ask each child to hold an end of ribbon as prayers are said, both of thanksgiving and for the needs of the world.

Give each child a 'living' sphere (e.g. a tomato, a pea, an orange, a melon) to hold. Ask each child to say thank you to God for the thing they are holding. Finish with prayers of thanksgiving for the wonders of the world.

Stars

Introduction

This theme is particularly suitable for use at Christmas, though it can be adapted for use at other times of the year. It can be closely linked to the previous two themes.

Setting

If possible, darken the room or use an alcove.

WALLS

Cover them with black paper or dark drapes decorated with different kinds of stars. Also use posters of the night sky and stars in space.

TABLE

Cover it with a dark cloth and place on it binoculars, a telescope and kaleidoscopes.

CHRISTMAS TREE

Decorate it with white lights (twinkling if possible), white decorations and silver and white stars.

CEILING

If possible, suspend from it some large black umbrellas with silver stars hanging from the spokes.

Sharing

When you've been out at night and looked into the sky, what did you see? How many stars did you see? How many do you think there are? Did you notice the patterns? Here's one called the Plough (show a large picture made from silver stars on a black background). The two end stars point to another star called the Pole Star (add the Pole Star using a bigger star). The Pole star helps sailors, travellers and people who live in the desert to find their way.

Play

Make the room as dark as possible (preparing the children sensitively) or use a dark but safe area (e.g. the stage with the curtains drawn, or trestle tables covered with blankets). Ask the children to follow a leader carrying a small lit torch up high, pointing towards the children.

Bible story
MATTHEW 2. 1–10

'There's something strange here,' said Caspar, looking through his telescope at the stars. 'Come and look'.

Melchior was just as surprised. 'I think it's a new star, a very bright one,' he said. 'Balthazar, come and look. What do you think?'

Balthazar was very old and wise. He knew that this was the special star that he had been waiting for all his life. He was very excited. He told the others, 'This star is very special. It means that a new king will be born. I must go to find him.'

'You're not going without us,' said the others. 'We're coming too.'

They did not know how long the journey was going to be, so they packed their bags, collected food for the journey, and climbed on their camels. They set off, as it got dark, to follow the star. Every day they rested. Every night they rode their camels, following the special, bright, shining star.

After days and weeks of travelling they came to the big city of Jerusalem. It was dawn, and Melchior could see a great, royal palace on the hill. 'That must be the place where the new king is,' he said. 'Let's go and find him.'

The three wise men were taken to see King Herod. They told him their story. He was very surprised and sent for his own wise men. They looked through all their books and found that there was a story that a baby would be born in Bethlehem who would become a king. King Herod said, 'If you find the new king, come back and tell us.'

That night, as it got dark, the wise men discovered that the star had moved on towards Bethlehem. They got more and more excited as they came nearer to the little town. 'This must be the place,' said Caspar, 'but where do we start looking for the baby?' Suddenly they heard a sound in the quiet of the night. It was a baby crying.

Activities

COLLAGE

Give each child a star-shaped piece of black paper. Provide a selection of silver paper, silver paint, silver crayons, silver fabric, silver felt tips, silver metallic paper, foil, sequins, sequin waste (punchinella) etc. Encourage the children to cut and tear the materials and to decorate the star shapes in their own way. These can then be fastened to the dark paper or drapes on the wall.

BISCUITS

Make biscuits cut with star biscuit cutters (see Appendix). Decorate with silver balls using melted white chocolate or ready-mixed white icing.

SPARKLERS

Light some sparklers and sing 'A special star' (*BBP*).

Music and rhymes

SONGS

'A special star, a special star' (*BBP*)

'Noel, noel, noel' (1st and 3rd verses) (*BBP*)

'See the star' (*Children's Praise*)

'Twinkle, twinkle little star' (*Someone's Singing, Lord*)

'God who put the stars in space' (*Sing and Pray*)

RHYMES

Can you count the stars?
As you look up there on high?
They twinkle all around us
Filling the midnight sky.

I'd really like to count them,
Find a name for every one,
I need someone to help me,
We could have such fun.

Stars alone and stars in clusters,
Twinkle on a clear dark night,
Forming shapes and pretty patterns
Showing off their special light.

Sparkling,
Glinting,
Glittering,
Glowing,
Stars in the night.
Twinkling,
Flickering,
Flashing,
Flowing.
Stars in the night.

Drama and movement

Encourage the children to make movements which are like still stars, shooting stars and, as a group, clusters of stars.

Another story

Questions, questions, questions and more questions. Mark was a boy who was always asking questions. One night he looked out of the window and saw the sun like a huge red ball beginning to disappear behind the hills as it began to get dark. Out of another window he saw the moon, like a round silver ball, sailing across the sky.

'Why do we need the sun?' Mark asked his Gran.

'Well, we need it for light in the day and to keep us warm,' replied Gran.

'And what's the moon for?' was his next question.

'Quite a lot of things actually,' said Gran. 'You'll learn about them when you are bigger. Some nights the moonlight is bright enough to see by.'

'What about the stars, then? What are they for? Starlight isn't very bright, is it?'

'There are millions of stars,' explained his Gran. 'I don't know anything about most of them, but there are some stars that seem to make a pattern, and people can use them to find their way.'

Just before Mark went to bed Gran said, 'It's dark now. Shall we go out and see if there are any stars tonight?' They went out and there wasn't a cloud in the sky, but there were lots of sparkling stars and some of them made patterns. Among them was one very bright star, all on its own.

'Gran, do you think that was the star the wise men saw that led them to the baby?'

'I don't know,' said Gran, 'but I do know that stars still lead people where they want to go.'

Story books

- Emilie Boon, *Peterkin Meets a Star*, Little Mammoth, 1993.
- Francesca Bosca, *Caspar and the Star*, Lion, 1991.
- Daniel Hochstatter, *Sammy Searches for Shapes and Sizes*, Nelson, 1994.

Prayers

Gather together in groups, each group under a star-filled black umbrella. Close your eyes and think of a sky without stars. Open your eyes and look at the stars around. Say thank you to God all together.

Presents

Introduction

It is possible to link this theme with the three previous ones and to use it for Epiphany.

Setting

Arrange the room to look as exciting as possible. Use Christmas and/or birthday wrappings and materials as appropriate.

ON THE WALLS

Pieces of wrapping paper, used wrapping paper cut into parcel shapes and decorated with ribbons and bows.

ROUND THE TREE OR ON A TABLE

Wrap Christmas/birthday parcels of all sizes in bright paper and decorate with ribbons. Add flowers or a plant wrapped in cellophane, a brown paper parcel and a padded envelope.

ON ANOTHER TABLE

Gift catalogues, empty boxes of different sizes, paper, ribbons, sellotape, scissors, tags, bows, string.

IN A SACK

Mystery parcels of assorted shapes, smells, sounds and feel.

Sharing

Encourage the children to guess what is in the different parcels, particularly those with strange shapes, smells, sounds and feel. Then ask the following questions: Who might they be for? Who do you give presents to? Why? Who has been to buy a present? Where did you go? What did you buy? Who did you buy the present for? Why do we give presents?

Play

Use all the things in the setting to pack 'pretend' parcels. Put them round the tree.

Bible stories

(Choose whichever one is appropriate in your situation.)

MATTHEW 2. 9–11

Listen. Can you hear a baby crying? Melchior, Caspar and Balthazar stopped quite still. The star they had been following was right overhead. This must be the place where they would find the baby king. But it was only a stable. As well as the baby's cries they could hear animals breathing and a gentle mooing. Then they heard a woman singing. (*Sing 'Sleep, sleep, gently sleep' (BBP) or another lullaby. Get the children to join in as they get to know it.*) As Mary sang, the baby grew quiet. It seemed as if the animals were listening as well.

'This must be the place,' said Caspar.

'It seems as if the special star has brought us to a special stable,' said Balthazar.

'Let's go in,' said Melchior,'and let's take the presents we have brought with us for the new king.'

The wise men went into the stable. They knelt down in front of the baby king. They gave him their presents. Do you know what they were?

MARK 12. 41–44

'This is a good spot to get out of the sun,' said Peter. It was a really hot afternoon. Jesus and his friends were sitting in one of the cool shady porches around the Temple in

Jerusalem. This was like a big church. There was so much to see and so many people passing by. Some of them were hurrying along to be in and out of the Temple quickly. Others were taking their time, and a few people seemed to be visiting the Temple for the first time. They kept stopping to look at the wonderful building or out at the view across the city.

Near where Jesus and his friends sat, there was a row of round tubs, rather like huge collecting boxes, where people put their money in for the Temple. Because these were made of metal, the coins really rattled as they went in.

There were some people who were dressed in grand clothes. They seemed to be trying to make as much noise as possible as they tossed in their money. There were other people who dropped their money in more gently.

Jesus noticed a woman coming in slowly by herself. She didn't have very grand clothes – in fact she looked quite poor. She stood quietly by the tub at the end of the row, and there was a soft tinkling noise as she dropped in two tiny coins. Then she went on into the Temple.

'Now look at that,' said Jesus to his friends. 'That lady is very poor. Some of the people gave a present of a lot of money, but they had a lot left over. The woman's present was very small, but it was all she had.'

 Activities

- Play 'Pass the Parcel'. [P]
- Share with the children the idea of giving gifts to some church members. Show them the gifts which have been bought. Ask them to guess which is for whom. Get the children to wrap the gifts. [P].
- Encourage every child to make a tag or gift card to fasten to the parcels. Pinking shears may be helpful, if they are not too stiff and big (look out for 'crazy cutters' which give different edges from pinking shears).

 ## Music and rhymes

SONGS

'Sleep, sleep, gently sleep' (*BBP*)

'Noel, noel' (*BBP*)

RHYMES

Jack in the box jumps up like this.
He makes me laugh as he waggles his head.
I gently press him down again
Saying, 'Jack-in-the-box you must go to bed.'

HPPA

Here is a box, here is a lid,
I wonder what inside is hid.
Why, it's a ... without a doubt.
Open the lid and let it pop out.

HPPA

(*Mime opening the lid. Give clues to what is inside the box (e.g. shape, colour, texture, what it's used for, what it rhymes with, or the noise it makes).*)

Surprises are round
Or long and tallish.
Surprises are square
Or flat and smallish.

Surprises are wrapped
With paper and bow,

95

And hidden in closets
Where secrets won't show.

Surprises are often
Good things to eat;
A get-well toy or
A birthday treat.

Surprises come
In such interesting sizes –
I LIKE
SURPRISES!

Jean Condor Soule in Another Very First Poetry Book

Drama and movement

Mime carrying presents of different kinds: very large, very small, very heavy, big and light, small and heavy, long and thin, short and fat.

Another story

A SPECIAL PARCEL

This is a true story, told by a dad:

'I don't know what I was expecting, the night my son was born. We were certainly looking forward to him coming. But we were worried that he was coming so soon. Two months early. So there were lots of doctors and nurses around to help.

'And when he did arrive, it all happened rather quickly. I was shown into a waiting room, where I sat and bit my finger nails and talked to two friends who had come to be with me.

'Ten minutes later the doctor came to find me. "You have a baby boy. And he's fine. Would you like to come and see him?"

'The doctor led me out of the waiting room, along a corridor and into another room where there was an incubator. Inside the incubator was what looked like a small package, not much bigger than a bag of sugar. The package was loosely wrapped in tin foil for warmth. Near one end, you could just see a little wrinkled red face, eyes tightly closed.

'This was my son, the first time I saw him. He's called Joe. We love him very much. And nowadays we don't wrap him in tin foil. He wears Manchester United kit and plays football in the garden after school.'

David Gamble

Story books

- Arthur Scholey, *Baboushka*, Lion, 1982.
- Shirley Hughes, *Giving*, Walker Books, 1995.
- Mick Inkpen, *Kipper's Birthday*, Hodder, 1994.

Prayers

Prepare a wrapped 'prayer parcel'. Fill a box with symbols to represent things to thank God for (e.g. a plant, a food item, a toy, a picture of a family). Ask the children to unpack the box and to pray for each in turn.

Preparation

Think in advance of three or four people from the church community who are known to the children and to whom it would be appropriate for the children to give inexpensive gifts. If possible, go with another leader and several children from the group to buy the gifts.

Prepare a parcel for 'Pass the parcel'.

Fruit

Aim

To give children the opportunity to discover the variety of fruits in God's world and to be grateful for those who help to provide them.

Setting

- Fresh fruit – apples, pears, bananas, grapes (essential), pineapples, mangos, kiwi fruit, oranges, lemons, grapefruit, starfruit, fruit in season etc. Some of the fruit should be cut up.
- Dried fruit – prunes, raisins, dates, apples, sultanas, apricots etc.
- Crystalised fruit – glacé cherries or pineapple (available at health food shops).
- Fruit juice – apple, orange, blackcurrant etc.
- A jug for the fruit juice, and some plastic tumblers.
- Tins of fruit to make fruit salad.
- Jars of marmalade and jam.
- Fruit cake, Christmas pudding, apple pie (some available for eating).
- Frozen fruit.
- Pictures or posters of fruit (sometimes available from fruit shops and from garden catalogues).
- Household items which portray fruit (e.g. tea towels, aprons, oven gloves).
- A lemon squeezer, a segment squeezer, an electric juicer, an apple corer, a potato peeler, a fruit knife, a grapefruit knife, a grater, a tin opener.

Sharing

How many kinds of fruit can you think of? Which are your favourites? Where does fruit grow? Which fruit have you seen growing? Which ones grow low to the ground, a bit higher or on high trees? In what ways do we use fruit?

Play

Look at, handle, smell and taste the fruit in the setting. Talk about how it tastes, smells and feels. Compare the same fruit when fresh, dried, as juice or frozen.

Bible story

NUMBERS 13. 20–23

A very long time ago, there were some people who didn't have houses to live in. They lived in tents and kept putting them up for a few weeks and then taking them down to move on to somewhere else. They were looking for a really good place where they could settle down and build themselves houses, and start gardens and farms to grow the food they needed, and where there was grass for their sheep and goats too.

As you can guess, they got rather tired and fed up with all this moving, so one day their leader, who was called Moses, suggested that they didn't all need to go on over the next hills to see what it was like there. 'We can ask a few people to go on ahead of the rest of us to find out about the place, then they can come back and tell us all about it.'

So a few men set out. The others waved goodbye to them, saying, 'Don't just come back with stories about what you've seen; bring back something you've found there to show us – then we'll know whether it would be a good place where we could settle down. We'll be looking out for you.'

Every day they made sure there was a lookout for the men coming back. This went on for a few weeks, so people started getting worried. But Moses told them not to worry. 'I'm sure we'll get good news soon,' he said.

Then one evening, just as it began to get dark, there was a shout from Amos, who was on lookout duty. 'I think I can see people coming down the hill towards us! They are walking quite slowly and they seem to be carrying things.' Everyone ran out to meet the men, who were tired and hot and dusty, but quite excited.

'Look what we found over those hills – a lovely green valley with plenty growing there. We've brought back some fruit we picked there, for you to see. Pomegranates and figs in this basket, and a huge bunch of grapes that we've carried carefully, hanging from a pole. It's a good place. We could settle happily there.'

Before they ate the fruit, Moses said a prayer. 'We must all thank God for this place where we are going to live.'

Activities

- Make a fruit salad.
- Blindfold children and get them to guess a particular fruit, first by smell, then by taste.
- Make a pomander in each small group. Make the holes in the orange in advance. Provide cloves for the children to place in the holes. Explain that they were used to make a pleasant smell in the days before aerosol sprays.
- Make a fruit porcupine using a cut potato. Supply cocktail sticks and a variety of suitable fresh, dried and glacé fruit for the children to thread on to the sticks and place in the potato. Share with as many adults as possible after the session.
- Make a fruit tree. Use a tree branch. Use pink and white collage to make blosssom for the branch, or fruit-coloured paints on to cardboard fruit shapes.

Music and rhymes

SONG

'Just a tiny seed' (*BBP*)

RHYME

Peach, peach
Some for each.
Cherry, cherry
Some for Terry.
Plum, plum,
Some for mum.
Pear, pear
More to share.
Kiwi, kiwi,
Some for me-me!

Drama and movement

- Mime eating different fruits (e.g. banana, grapes, cherries, apple) and get others to guess which fruit it is.
- Pretend to be a tiny seed growing into a large tree, then growing blossoms and fruit.
- Act out harvesting fruit of different kinds (e.g. strawberries, gooseberries, apples).
- Play 'Oranges and Lemons'.

Another story

I wonder if you like strawberries. We usually have them in the summer and often they are a special treat. Do you know how they grow and how they get on your plate?

Strawberries grow on plants that creep out along the ground, from their roots. So if you are going to pick them, you have to keep bending over to feel under the leaves to find ones that are nearly red and ripe. Some people grow strawberries in their gardens and they can pick some each day, when they want to eat them. But lots of strawberries grow in long rows out in the fields, and people can spend a whole day at a time, just picking strawberries.

David had a strawberry farm. Every summer his brother Rick, and Rick's friends from college, came to camp in tents in the corner of the strawberry field. They stayed for a few weeks, and if it wasn't raining, they picked strawberries all day long, starting early in the morning before it got too hot. Rick and Keith and John and Mike and Bayo and the others collected empty baskets and began picking strawberries along the long rows. At first, they walked along, bending over the plants to find the best strawberries to put in the baskets. Later on they sat on the ground between the rows of plants and shuffled along as they picked, or they knelt down and crawled along. Later on still, when they were getting really tired, they even lay down to pick!

The good thing was that sometimes they could eat a juicy strawberry that would go soft if it was put in the basket. When the baskets were full, they had to be carried over to the table to be weighed and then to be packed on to the lorry that took the strawberries to the market and the shops.

Everyone could carry two full baskets of strawberries, one in each hand. Rick had big strong hands and he could carry two in each hand. But best of all was Bayo – he could carry two baskets in each hand and five baskets on his head, balanced on his thick, black, curly hair! He came from Nigeria where people often carry their shopping or their school books on their heads. The others tried hard to copy him (but not with full baskets of straw-

berries), but they couldn't do it. I wonder if you could carry something on your head. Please don't try with strawberries!

Story books

- Janet and Alan Ahlberg, *Each Peach, Pear, Plum*, Picture Lions, 1980.
- Judith Bennet Richardson, *The Way Home*, Red Fox, 1980.
- Eric Carle, *The Very Hungry Caterpillar*, Picture Puffin, 1974.

Prayers

Place a basket of fruit in the centre of the group. Ask each child to collect an item from the setting to hold. Say a thank-you prayer for all the different kinds of fruit. Say thank you for all the people who have helped to provide the fruit:

- The farmer who looks after the land.
- The fruit grower who cares for the orchard.
- The gardener who digs and plants.
- The pickers who work in the fields and orchards.
- The lorry driver who brings boxes to the shop.
- The pilot who flies aeroplanes with fruit from other countries.
- The captain whose ship brings more fruit.
- The shopkeeper who collects it from the market.
- The shop assistant who piles it up to look beautiful.
- The mummies and daddies who buy the fruit and bring it home for us to eat.

Appendix

Meringue
(microwave recipe)

- Use: 1 egg white, 300 g (12 oz) sieved icing sugar.
- Put the egg white in a mixing bowl. Mix in icing sugar to make a stiff mixture. Roll into small balls, the size of a marble.
- Arrange the balls, 4 at a time, well apart on kitchen paper on a large plate. Microwave for about $1\frac{1}{4}$ minutes. Repeat using a cold plate and fresh kitchen paper.

Star biscuits

- Use: 50g (2 oz) sugar, 50g (2 oz) margarine, 100g (4 oz) plain flour, 1 beaten egg, flavouring ($\frac{1}{4}$ tsp cinnamon, or $\frac{1}{2}$ tsp mixed spice, or 1 tsp lemon juice).
- Cream the margarine and sugar together. Add the flour and egg alternately, and the flavouring. Knead to a smooth mix and roll out on a floured board. Cut with a star cutter. Cook at 350F, 170C or Gas mark 5 for 10 minutes.

Truffles

- Use: 10 digestive biscuits, 5 level tablespoons coconut, 5 level tablespoons drinking chocolate, 1 small can condensed milk, 50g (2 oz) melted margarine, chocolate vermicelli for decoration.
- Place the biscuits in a plastic bag and crush them with a rolling pin. Mix all the ingredients together (except the vermicelli) and form into balls. Roll in the chocolate vermicelli. Place in paper cases and leave to set. Makes 15-20 truffles.

Cooked dough

- Use: 2 cups of flour, 1 cup of salt, 2 cups of water, 2 tablespoons of oil, 2 teaspoons of cream of tartar.
- Cook the mixture in a pan over a medium heat, stirring all the time to prevent sticking. Remove from the heat when the mixture comes away from the side of the pan. Knead well. This will store in an air-tight container for a long time. If required, the mixture can be cooked. Once modelled, bake it until thoroughly dried out. Paint after cooking.
- (Note: If the models are to be permanent, paint them with a coat of clear varnish.)

Microwave dough

- Use: 4 cups plain flour, 1 cup salt, $1\frac{1}{2}$ cups water.
- Optional: ready-mixed paint (if you use this, add a little extra flour).
- Mix the flour and salt together. Stir in one cup of water. Knead well. Add the remaining water as needed. Knead into a pliable dough. Add paint if wished.
- Roll out. Mould or cut. Place on a lightly oiled microwave-safe plate. Bake on medium (microwave) power for about 12 minutes, checking at 2-minute intervals until the surfaces are hard. Leave for 15 minutes. Decorate.

Christingles

For each orange (representing the world):

- Make a hole in the top. Fill it with foil which overlaps (to reflect the light of Jesus).
- Put a small candle into the foil-lined hole (the light of Jesus).
- Fasten a red ribbon round the orange (Jesus died for the whole world).
- Provide cocktail sticks, small sweets, dolly mixtures, jelly tots, sultanas, raisins, pieces of date, maraschino cherries etc. Thread these onto four cocktail sticks (representing north, south, east and west).
- Place them in the orange (the fruits of the earth).

An Easter garden

Encourage the children to use the materials to express their own ideas:

- A tray or large plate of damp compost/fibre (not peat).
- A small tin lid to hold water, a small mirror or foil for the pool or stream.
- Moss, bark, small stones, pebbles etc.
- Twigs, tiny plants, seedlings, etc.

Or:

- A tray or large plate lined with green paper or fabric.
- A mirror or foil.
- Stones, pebbles, bark, twigs etc.
- Twigs (green tissue/crêpe paper, fabric etc. for leaves) stuck in plasticine or dough.

Artificial rain

To make artificial rain: lay lengths of cotton or thread on a polythene sheet or bag. Place blobs of PVA glue at intervals along the strands. Leave for a few hours to dry. Peel off carefully.

A scroll

Fasten two sheets of A4 paper together with sticky tape. Put lettering on, if wished. Soak in cold tea. Bake in a low oven until dry (15-20 minutes). Attach a strip of wood to each end. Roll up.

Welly walking

Provide a wide variety of welly boots in different sizes. Cover the floor with plastic or go outside if possible. Place Spontex washing-up cloths in the bottom of a large baking tray (or turkey tin). Cover with half an inch of brightly coloured paint (not mauve, which stains). Place at one end of long sheet of lining paper, or similar. At the other end place a large bowl of clean, soapy water and some drying cloths. Have fun!

Parachute games

Mushroom

Players stand equally spaced around the parachute, holding the edge. On the word 'down' the parachute is lowered to the ground, and on 'up' they raise their arms high in the air. Create rhythmic movements with the words 'up' and 'down'.

Change Over

With the parachute going up and down, call out a description, e.g. 'wearing blue'. Anyone wearing blue will drop hands and change places with another by running under the parachute.

Resources

Books

Children's Illustrated Bible, Dorling Kindersley, 1994

Come Follow Me, Evans Bros Ltd, 1966

Linda Hammond, *Five Furry Teddy Bears*, Penguin, 1990

Eileen Goddard, *See the Daisies, Feel the Rain*, GLPPA, 1978

John Foster (compiler) *Another Very First Poetry Book*, Oxford University Press, 1992

A.J. McCallen, *Listen*, Collins, 1976

A.J. McCallen, *Praise*, Collins, 1979

Elizabeth Matterson, *This Little Puffin*, Puffin Books, Penguin Books Ltd, 1969

Word Play, Finger Play, Pre-School Learning Alliance, 1985

Song books

Apusskidu, A. & C. Black, 1975

Big Blue Planet, Methodist Division of Education & Youth and Stainer & Bell, 1995

Children's Praise, Marshall Pickering, 1991

Come and Praise, BBC, 1990

Feeling Good, National Society/Church House Publishing, 1994

Jump Up If You're Wearing Red, National Society/Church House Publishing, 1996

Junior Pray, Marshall Pickering, 1986

Many and Great, Wild Goose, 1990

The Music Box Songbook, BBC, 1990

Okki Tokki Unga, A. & C. Black, 1976

Sing and Praise, Sunday School Society for Ireland, 1990

Someone's Singing, Lord, A. & C. Black, 1973

Tinder-box, A. & C. Black, 1982

Bible Index

Note: Most of these themes are usable at any season, but some suggestions are given.

Bible references	Content	Theme	Seasons	Page
1 Kings 17. 4–5	Elijah is fed by ravens	Black and white	Any	78
1 Kings 19. 12	Elijah and the 'still, small voice'	Sounds	Any	70
Acts 8. 26–39	Philip and the eunuch	Books	Any	2
Acts 27	Paul's shipwreck	Transport	Any	14
Exodus 2. 1–10	Moses in the bulrushes	New babies	Any	18
Genesis 1. 31	The Creation	Spheres	Christmas	86
Genesis 6. 9 – 8. 19	Noah's ark	Weather	Any	66
Genesis 37. 3	Joseph's coat of many colours	Colours	Any	74
John 13. 4–9	Washing the disciples' feet	Hands and feet	Any	30
John 20. 10–18	Mary meets the risen Christ	Garden centre	Easter	50
Judges 7. 2–7	Gideon tests the troops	Water is useful	Any	62
Judges 14. 8	'Out of strength came forth sweetness'	Mini-beasts	Any	54